The Deras

The Deras

Culture, Diversity and Politics

Foreword by MARK JUERGENSMEYER

SANTOSH K. SINGH

PENGUIN
VIKING
An imprint of Penguin Random House

VIKING

Viking is an imprint of the Penguin Random House group of companies whose addresses can be found at global.penguinrandomhouse.com

Published by Penguin Random House India Pvt. Ltd
4th Floor, Capital Tower 1, MG Road,
Gurugram 122 002, Haryana, India

Penguin Random House India

First published in Viking by Penguin Random House India 2025

10 9 8 7 6 5 4 3 2 1

ISBN 9780670098316

Typeset in RequiemText by Manipal Technologies Limited, Manipal
Printed at Replika Press Pvt. Ltd, India

www.penguin.co.in

MIX
Paper | Supporting responsible forestry
FSC™ C016779
FSC www.fsc.org

Contents

Foreword

The Power of Deras

'Do you want to go to the dera?' the young fellow in Jalandhar asked me.

'Of course,' I responded, knowing that the Sachkhand Dera in nearby Ballan was the epicentre of reverence for Ravidas, the fifteenth-century poet and saint who had become emblematic of the distinctive culture of the Scheduled Caste followers of Punjab's Ad-Dharm movement.

My research project focused on Ad-Dharm, a religious and political movement that attempted to reconceive the religious basis for social order in the early twentieth century so that members of the lower castes would not be marginalized. Unlike the caste hierarchy of Hindu society, it portrayed a spiritual landscape of egalitarian character, where a leather worker—like them—could be regarded as the patron saint. Their spiritual mentor, Ravidas, was not afraid to link his caste occupation to his spiritual pursuits, as this verse of his poetry indicates:

Oh well known of Benares,
I too am born well-known;
My labour is with leather,
But my heart can boast the Lord.[1]

I came across the Ad-Dharm movement quite by accident. When I was in graduate school at Berkeley, I rummaged through old British census tracts and found an item in the 1930 Census titled 'Revolt of the Untouchables'. It described a new movement that had created a religion called Ad-Dharm—the 'original religion'—as an alternative to Hinduism. The idea was for members of the Scheduled Castes in Punjab—some 25 per cent of the state's population—to identify as Ad-Dharm rather than as Sikh, Hindu or Muslim. They would thus create political leverage that would allow them to negotiate with the upper-caste leaders for better conditions for the Scheduled Castes. It was a clever idea, and a profound one, since it went to the heart of the religious character of Indian society. Social change required social vision. I decided this was just the sort of combination of religion and politics that I was looking for as a research topic for my dissertation, which also became my first published research book.[2]

Moreover, little had been written about the movement. This meant that rather than spending hours in musty archives, I would simply have to return to Punjab—where I had previously spent two years as a scholar in residence at Panjab University in the late sixties, and for which I had gained a certain fondness. I would have to ride on the back of a scooter to go to the dera that had hosted the first Ad-Dharm rally. And I would have to talk to people to hunt down any of the old Ad-Dharm leaders who might still be around when I returned in the early 1970s.

Fortunately, I was able to locate the founder of the movement, Mangoo Ram, who was then in his nineties. I found him sitting on a charpoy in his farm near the village of Mugowal in Hoshiarpur district. When I introduced myself, in my halting combination of Punjabi and Hindi, I told him I was from the University of California. 'California?' he said in English, 'I used to live in Fresno.'

Fresno is not one of the great urban centres of the state. But it is in the heart of the fertile agricultural fields of California's Central Valley, and it was there that young Mangoo Ram went to work in the orchards. Eventually, he joined the Ghadar Party, a revolutionary movement aimed at the overthrow of British rule in India, which was based in Northern California. Although Mangoo Ram was captured by British spies, he was eventually able to return to Punjab, where he decided that liberation had to begin with his own people. He set about launching a new movement for the betterment of people from the lower castes, such as himself.

He and his circle of politically astute colleagues decided to create a new religious identity that could rival the dominant Hindu, Sikh and Muslim leadership in Punjab. They realized that there was already a basis for religiosity among Scheduled Caste people that could serve as a focal point for this new religion. This led them to the long-standing reverence for the fifteenth-century poet-saint, Ravidas, and the dera at Ballan that was dedicated to him. Mangoo Ram's first rally for the creation of the Ad-Dharm movement was held on a ground adjacent to the dera.

In this interesting and wide-ranging book, Santosh K. Singh highlights the extraordinary influence that deras in Punjab have had on the character of Punjabi society, often intertwined with its politics. As he points out, the spiritual master of Dera Ballan at the time of Mangoo Ram's rally in the late 1920s, Sant Sarwan Das, was politically astute. He joined forces with Mangoo Ram, and the reverence for Ravidas took on a political as well as spiritual force.

When I first went to the Ballan dera, it was at the invitation of a young man from the Boota Mandi area of Jalandhar. His name was Manohar Mahey, and he later became a leading figure in the community as well as one of the main patrons of the dera. At the time, however, he was just a nice kid who was willing to help out this young Berkeley graduate student and allow him to ride on the back of his scooter as he drove to the nearby village of Ballan.

Manohar introduced me to the ageing master of the dera, Sant Sarwan Das. He had hosted Mangoo Ram's rally that created the Ad-Dharm movement forty years earlier. He continued to be a leader in the community, not just for religious enlightenment but also for social empowerment. He was a towering figure. He explained to me the origins of the Ballan dera, as I recorded in my book. When I met him, he was sitting by an electric fan, wearing sunglasses.[3] He had a flowing white beard and was dressed in an all-white version of the typical Punjabi kurta-shirt and pyjama-pants, topped with an orange turban. He explained that his father, Pipal Das, had been an adherent of the poet-saint, Ravidas, and later became a holy seeker of truth in the Ravidas tradition. At the beginning of the twentieth century, while wandering in search of truth, he came to a place with a pipal tree that initially appeared to be dead. On watering it, however, the tree sprang to life. Pipal Das understood this as a sign that this was the spot where he should encamp in his search for truth. Nearby villagers donated the land, and in time it became a pilgrimage site for those who venerated Ravidas and regarded

Pipal Das as a *sant* (saint) worthy of respect and admiration. Thus, the dera began.

The concept of a dera is an ancient one. The word relates to an encampment, and quite likely, the earliest deras were places where sadhus and other spiritual seekers would camp in the precincts of a spiritual master. Thus, a dera has several defining characteristics: it has a spiritual leader as the focal point, a group of followers who gather around him (or her, though almost all of the gurus at deras have been male) and a location where the master lives and the adherents can camp out, either temporarily or for a longer stay.

According to the great anthropologist Clifford Geertz, every society is grounded in a sense of a centre. Such centres are 'concentrated loci of serious acts', the arenas in a society 'where its leading ideas come together with its leading institutions', and 'where momentous events are thought to occur'.[4] They are a part of the charisma of leadership, and such centres are the logical locus for a spiritual master.

As Santosh K. Singh says in this brilliant and informative book, there are such centres—the deras—scattered throughout Punjab and elsewhere in north India. One of the largest is Dera Baba Jaimal Singh, the headquarters of the Beas branch of the Radha Soami tradition, located on the banks of the Beas River, halfway between Jalandhar and Amritsar. It is home to the spiritual master of the dera, which, after all, is the point of a dera: to encamp near the master. Although the leadership of the Radha Soami movement is largely from the merchant castes, the overwhelming percentage of the hundreds of thousands of villagers who come to the great festivals at Beas are from the lower castes, including many who also worship at the Ballan dera dedicated to Ravidas. For that reason, I included a chapter on Radha Soami in my book featuring the Ad-Dharm movement, and I later expanded that chapter into a full-length book.

Interestingly, the story that is told about the founding of the Radha Soami dera at Beas is strikingly similar to the one that Sarwan Das recounted about how his mentor, Pipal Das, founded the dera at Ballan. It was established by a soldier in the Indian Army who had encamped near Agra and visited the meditation grounds of the first guru in the Radha Soami tradition, Swami Shiv Dayal Singh. When he retired from military service, the soldier, Jaimal Singh, a Sikh from Punjab, returned to his home region and looked for a location where he could resume meditation, as instructed by his Radha Soami master. He found a lonely spot on the banks of the Beas River, but at first, it seemed a daunting locale. It was infested with snakes and other wild animals, and criminal gangs used the caves along the riverbank as hideouts. Nonetheless, Jaimal Singh was undeterred and established his camp, much as he had when he was in the Indian Army. However, he did not meditate alone for long. Disciples came to seek spiritual insights from him and to be initiated into the faith. They saw in him a living master, and thus the lineage of Beas masters was established. The dera he created has become a small city named after its founder, Dera Baba Jaimal Singh. Its adherents describe it as 'heaven on earth'.[5]

The Radha Soami tradition began in 1869, and at the death of a living master, there would inevitably be several contenders for the succession. Today, there are dozens of branches stemming from the original encampments at Agra and Beas, along with smaller deras related to Radha Soami throughout Punjab.[6] One of the more controversial of these is described accurately in this book. It is Dera Sacha Sauda, led by Gurmeet Ram Rahim, the so-called 'guru of bling', who has been implicated in fraud, sexual misconduct and murder charges. To the embarrassment of most Radha Soami adherents, the guru of bling falls legitimately within the Radha Soami lineage.

When the founder of the Beas dera, Jaimal Singh, died in 1903, he was succeeded by one of his disciples, Sawan Singh, whose tenure as the living master at Beas extended from 1903 to 1948. Dubbed 'the Great Master', it was thought that no one could quite succeed him. And in fact, no single individual did, but there were several contenders. Among them was Mastana Baluchistani, who had an interesting relationship with the Great Master. Apparently, he was allowed to perform initiations and lead a fellowship, authorized by the Great Master himself. Perhaps these dual master roles were fitting since Mastana operated in an area at some distance from Beas. Mastana was succeeded by Master Pita Shah, who surprised his followers by designating a young man, Gurmeet Ram Rahim, as his successor. Rahim, in addition to his alleged notorious dealings, has lived flamboyantly, dressing in outrageous outfits, singing in a rock band and performing in videos.

His was not the usual demeanour for Radha Soami masters and their followers. In general, deras are places of calm and meditation, with extended periods of peace punctuated only by the great festival occasions when thousands encamp to receive the darshan of the master. At Beas, the large *bhandara* festivals have grown to such a size that one master, Charan Singh, would give darshan blessings via television monitors set up throughout the tented structure where the crowds gathered. His successor, Gurinder, is driven around the throng, seated at the back of a truck, dispensing blessings as his admirers crowd around to see him.

When I conducted a survey of village religiosity, I was fascinated by the diversity expressed by the respondents.

Though many of them were committed disciples of Ravidas, whose picture hung in their humble homes, they also revered the master at Beas, whose picture sometimes hung alongside that of the fifteenth-century cobbler saint. They also worshipped at gurudwaras and at Hindu temples that allowed them to do so. The boundaries among different kinds of religiosity are not rigid, it seems. Thus, it is understandable that an outside observer might see only part of the picture. They may observe these individuals worshipping in gurudwaras and temples and think that they are securely part of the Sikh and Hindu religious communities. That, however, is only part of the story.

This facile understanding of religion in Punjab misses the importance of other types of religious associations that undercut the dominant forms of religious life. Worship of Ravidas and obeisance to the Radha Soami masters can be just as vital forms of religiosity, if not more so. The deras in Punjab are prominent focal points for these alternative religious communities. And as Santosh K. Singh illustrates in this readable and enlightening book, the deras can be formidable indeed.

16 October 2024

Mark Juergensmeyer
Distinguished Professor Emeritus of
Sociology and Global Studies,
University of California, Santa Barbara, USA

Preface

Notes of a Wanderer

For a trained sociologist, undertaking fieldwork is nothing extraordinary. With a research plan backed by an intensive review of the literature and a clear sense of methodological tools, a researcher is expected to hit the field like a fish takes to water. It is as if the field is an outside construct that has no agency, and it is the researcher who makes it come alive. Else it is dead or incognito. In other words, it is the researcher who gives the field an identity. On its own, the field is anonymous. A researcher's gaze makes the field relevant and worthy of documentation.

This imagination of the field and fieldwork is a colonial construct and clearly invests too much agency with the researcher. While there is a great tradition of such fieldwork, which gained prominence with the spread of colonialism in the eighteenth century, simultaneously, a muted history too came along—of stories, autobiographies, folklores and mythologies—that was sidelined, for the latter celebrated folk curiosity and its serendipity, which did not measure up to the standards of empiricism that demanded more factual, quantifiable and consistent data. The voices, experiences and encounters that were not part of any research design and lacked empiricist methodological sophistication found less favour with the knowledge industry that emerged over time. Gradually, academic research endeavours became heavily loaded with tools, techniques and its controlled regime and template. In this politics of knowledge creation and the resultant industry that emerged, the biggest casualty turned out to be the element of 'curiosity'.

The strictly regimented world of academic research that compels its seekers to first choose the techniques and then appreciate and pursue the idea of being curious about a theme tends to create a soulless world of robotic research. Knowledge in its true and pure sense is like a beautiful bird perched on the branch of a tree that is beheld by a curious seeker, who is enchanted by the ambience. A Newton today therefore must first learn to sit quietly under a tree and appreciate the hanging apples. Theories will emerge following that curious engagement with one's surroundings.

This book is a culmination of a series of journeys marked by almost magical, serendipitous moments and encounters. And serendipity, one realizes, is the hallmark of a research journey undertaken in curiosity and emerging from enchantment with the space under investigation. This is unlike the routine fieldwork that an academic engages with or in. The notion of 'field' has an overdose of control, planning and standardized methods in its matrix as exercised by the researcher. Also, it is largely an exercise in othering and subject-making. The idea of fieldwork that became a trademark tool of investigation and research in anthropology and sociology in the early centuries of colonialism, despite all its reflexivity later, remained true and committed to its primary objective—to study the 'other'. While this method might have worked in many research undertakings—several of which are iconic—when it comes to a space as fluid and emotive as religion, that too in the landscape of South Asia, especially Punjab, the standard fieldwork template appears to be a misfit.

Wandering as a craft, as an idea, is valuable for its flexibility and reflexivity. The best part is that it creates a synergy and symbiosis between the researcher and the researched. The field is no more an inert idea waiting to be explored and revived; rather, both the field and the researcher remake each other in the course of the journey. A new twist, a new narrative, a new encounter—all carry the possibility and potential of reimagining the research trajectory and its questions. In our world, the great travellers and wanderers like Nanak, Buddha, Ravidas and then Gandhi were wanderer-philosophers whose world views were shaped primarily by the 'field'. The transformation of Siddhartha to Gautam Buddha and his enlightenment happened because of the field called society and its people, through a dialogue between the field and the researcher.

Two encounters

My doctoral work was on agrarian questions, and hence as a natural progression, I was conditioned to believe that my research would be around themes concerning rural societies. While teaching in Chandigarh, I applied for a grant to conduct a research project on agribusiness in villages in Punjab. My proposal was approved, and I received a major research grant. For about six months in 2009, we conducted fieldwork. However, the project soon had to be shelved as I had to leave for Delhi to join a newly founded social sciences university, and the rules of the funding agency did not allow the project to be transferred to the new university (as it did not qualify to receive the grant money). So with a heavy heart, I had to shut down the project. Around that time, newspapers in Punjab were replete with news of a religious organization known as the Dera Sacha Sauda, headed by a person called Ram Rahim. Frequent mention was made of the organization's aggressive stance and mass mobilization. The dera was constantly in the midst of one controversy or the other and had a strained relationship with the Sikh *panth* bodies, which were at the helm of religious affairs among the Sikh community.

Although I had shelved the agribusiness project, I remembered that a large part of the workforce on the farms was from the Dalit community. But this was not unusual. What struck me was that many of them wore a locket around their necks embossed with the insignia of Ram Rahim's Sacha Sauda. It was something that stayed with me. Ram Rahim and those lockets sparked my curiosity. I was filled with the excitement to explore further. What explained this connection? Was I missing something?

What followed thereafter was a more-than-decade-long engagement with the phenomenon of the *dera*. Deras are, simply speaking, a place of worship and congregation around a sacred person or Guru. Like the Dera Sacha Sauda, there were other deras. While I still teach courses on rural matters at my university, my research pursuits have largely been around the institution of the dera. This not only took me to various parts of Punjab and to many deras, but it also connected me to Varanasi, the place where the Ravidassia community, led by Dera Ballan of Punjab, built a pilgrimage centre at the birthplace of Guru Ravidas, the Bhakti poet and sant.

It is during this period of my transition from Chandigarh to Delhi that I experienced another significant moment, which only added to my curiosity and spurred me to continue my research pursuit more resolutely.

The non-AC coach of the Delhi–Chandigarh Jan Shatabdi Express was relatively crowded that day. Barring me and a few others, it was occupied largely by members of a religious group who, as I found out later, had come from Chandigarh to attend a Nirankari satsang* in Delhi and were now returning. My co-passenger, Ram Swaroop, sixty-eight, was also a member of the Nirankari group. The casual conversation that we had struck up at the Delhi station continued till we reached Chandigarh, interrupted occasionally by a chaiwallah. In the span of just about four hours, a brief history of more than four decades of migration, conversion, displacement and the knotty rehabilitation of a community was narrated.

Ram Swaroop and a few others, all belonging to the untouchable Chamar caste, had migrated to Chandigarh with their families in the 1960s from Rae Bareilly in Uttar Pradesh. The city was being planned and constructed at the time, and consequently, a large labour force from neighbouring states had made their way there. Nothing extraordinary happened to Ram Swaroop in Chandigarh, except that he was able to lead a life of dignity and honour in the city, which he spoke of with much gratitude.

It was in Chandigarh that Swaroop and many others from his community came in contact with the Nirankaris and became members of this group. They continued to worship Guru Ravidas, the fifteenth-century Bhakti saint and poet and their traditional deity, as their new homeland and its great syncretic tradition gave them enough space to accommodate and engage with their past. Ram Swaroop retained his connection with his

* Nirankaris are a prominent sect within Sikhism.

roots but was saddened that not much had changed in his old home, as caste lines remained rigid and divisive. He shared with me a community song in his local dialect, which I present here verbatim as I dedicate this book to him and his community. The song is full of pathos and expresses the community's anguish about the wretched caste hierarchy:

Chhui pae na basanma,
Hame kaun manai.
Ek hai suraj chand sitare
Ek hai Aaasmaan,
Ek hai sab ma haad maas hai,
Ek hai Bhagwan.
Kahe ham pe hi doswa lagaya babua
Kahe Harijan, Acchutwa
Banaya Babua.
Chhui pae na basanma
Hame kaun manai.
Who will believe us,
Cannot even touch your utensils.
There is one sun, there is one moon
Even the sky is one.
Our body too is the same with the same flesh and bones
But why do you blame us for everything?
Why did you make us different?
Why did you call us untouchable and Harjan?[1]

These two experiences, I must admit, motivated me to pursue an in-depth investigation into the idea of the dera. What followed was more than a decade of wandering to various deras in Punjab which eventually also connected me to the city of Varanasi in Uttar Pradesh. The high point was a train journey in the Begampura Express from Jalandhar in Punjab to Varanasi on the occasion of Guru Ravidas Jayanti, the birth anniversary of Guru Ravidas, which is usually celebrated in the beginning of a new year, around February, on Magh Purnima, the full moon day in the Hindu month of Magh. This overnight journey in an ordinary sleeper class was remarkable and enriching in terms of the kind of stories and experiences that were shared by my co-travellers. The whole experience was surreal. Most of my visits to Varanasi were on the occasion of Ravidas Jayanti, as that was when I was able to meet a large number of non-resident Indians, who form a significant part of the movement around Guru Ravidas.

On other occasions, I travelled to meet the leaders of other communities, like the Valmikis of Jalandhar, the factions of various deras in different parts of the state, parallel organizations in conflict with the Dera Ballan and its Varanasi Project and so on. Since my focus was on the Ravidassia movement as led by the Dera Sachkhand Ballan, I devoted more time to the Ballan group and its functionaries. Given the pivotal role that this dera has played, it was only natural that it remained the focus of my wanderings in the sense that I kept returning to Ballan, which included one visit with the legendary Berkeley professor, Mark Juergensmeyer, who had conducted the first serious research work on the Dera Ballan and the Ravidassia community way back in the 1970s. During a chance meeting in Delhi, I learnt that he would be travelling to Jalandhar to meet the respondents from that study. I simply piled on and travelled with him wherever he went to meet people, observe people, dine with community leaders and be part of the enriching conversations that followed. It was on this trip that I met Manohar Lal Mahey, who had assisted and accompanied Professor Juergensmeyer during his visits. The conversations that I had with veteran scholar and intellectual L.R. Balley on this trip facilitated my meeting with him later, when we spent a day leisurely talking at his residence in Jalandhar, about his leader and mentor Dr B.R. Ambedkar and his Buddhist orientation. In a similar vein, I was also introduced to Paramjit Singh Kainth, a firebrand grassroots leader from Patiala.

Based on these serendipitous meetings with three different individuals from a similar subaltern political background but with entirely contrasting world views and political missions, I subsequently wrote an academic article in a journal that was widely circulated among both practitioners of sociology and activists.[2] None of these meetings were planned. They happened on their own as my wandering, spurred by sheer curiosity to meet people, visit places and connect the dots, continued. One thing led to another. One visit to a dera led to another. Varanasi happened because of Jalandhar, and it exposed me to a much larger canvas, making me realize that, to understand Jalandhar, it was essential to visit Varanasi. It was through this complex and messy labyrinth of diverse, criss-crossing pathways that the bigger picture of the Ravidassia movement emerged to eclipse the localized world of a Ram Rahim.

The phenomenon of the dera was further illuminated as my wandering continued. Interestingly, Ram Rahim and his dera have remained in the news, continuing to grab the limelight even today. In fact, people's interest in the dera phenomenon is periodically enlivened by his mercurial and strange but colourful ways. So much so that even though he is currently in jail, he continues to call the shots and stay relevant. His presence in the mass media has been so powerful and consistent that a large number of people perceive him and his organization as the representational prototype dera.

This, I believe, is a gross misrepresentation. Dera culture in northwest India, especially in Punjab, has an ancient history, and it stands on a philosophically rich swathe of expansive terra firma. To reduce this lengthy and complex history to a tiny spot is not just a historical misrepresentation of a great tradition but also misinformation that maligns a rich tradition of philosophical argumentation and counter-perspectives. Deras reflect South Asia's fluid sacred geography and its propensity to constantly and seamlessly engage in multiple conversations with each other.

This book is, therefore, a modest effort to rescue the fascinating, deeply philosophical and emancipatory realm of deras from being boxed in a narrow, sectarian and parochial framework. Deras are not just complex institutions; they also carry a rich diversity of histories encompassing time, people and communities that seamlessly draw from the past and negotiate with the present to carve out a new future.

It is against this backdrop that the book begins with the story of a village to highlight the everyday nature of Punjab's syncretic and multi-religious cultural mould—a reminder of what is so organic and inherent in our world. The first chapter is a precursor to the world of deras that in contemporary times have become contest-ridden and have fallen victim to the politics of identity. This chapter is followed by a conceptual background of the phenomenon of the dera and its connection with caste. After a short, descriptive and a largely secondary source-based chapter on Dera Sacha Sauda and Ram Rahim, the book explores its core theme through a more substantive, primary first-hand account of the Dera Sachkhand Ballan, its politics, pilgrimages, diaspora and strained relationships with some of its own. The most remarkable part is the story of how this dera emerged from a quiet, ordinary place in Ballan village to become a global centre of Ravidassia identity articulation. Its national aspirations, combined with a chequered history of internal churning, contestations and conflict with various factions, present a fascinating account of the dynamic and diverse world of deras, their culture and politics.

Finally, I circle back to another wanderer's account, where a traveller, equipped with his sociological imagination, engages in dialogue with the people and their stories, myths and histories to explore the possibility of opening a window into South Asia's contemporary religious landscape, especially for its youth. 'Why youth?' one could understandably ask. There is an anecdote that answers this.

A few years ago, during a morning walk with my teenage son in Delhi, we encountered a sight that was ordinary to me but awe-inspiring for him. A group of Jain devotees were walking barefoot, encircling a religious figure who wasn't wearing any clothes. My son was flabbergasted by the nudity and its public display. It took me a while to explain to him the profound philosophy of asceticism and the concept of nothingness enshrined in Jainism, as represented in what he thought was merely crass nudity. As he began to understand these concepts, he looked more at ease and, eventually, at peace.

Religion is here to stay. The message of connectedness, syncretism and exchange must therefore be communicated to young minds so they become less judgemental and are encouraged to delve deeper into philosophical questions and meanings—the kernel that constitutes the South Asian religious landscape.

1

The Story of a Village in Punjab: Mapping the Sacred Geography*

A village named Gehuan

The village of Gehuan,* like many Indian villages, carries an inflated sense of itself, particularly of its antiquity. A rich repertoire of stories, legends, myths and histories is unleashed following an ordinary enquiry about the past of the village. The interesting part, however, is the uniformity with which these renditions are shared by various segments of the society, across faiths and castes. Tucked in a corner of one of the neighbouring districts of the city of Chandigarh, almost on the highway connecting Punjab with Himachal Pradesh, Gehuan is locally known for its mythical pond, believed to have been built by the Pandavas of the Mahabharata during their thirteen-year *vanavaas* or period of exile in the forest. This bit of the past is invariably the beginning of all conversations regarding the history of the village, irrespective of whether the villager is a Sikh, Hindu or Muslim.

---

* Following standard anthropological tradition, a pseudonym has been used.

One legend holds that the name of the village came from Ghatotkach, the son of the mighty Pandava Bhim, and Hidimba. The village is also considered a sacred site as the Sikh gurus visited this place, and there are gurudwaras to commemorate their arrival. Gehuan is also known for its artisanal work, especially blacksmith work, a tradition carried on by a few households of Sikh *lohars*, who specialize in moulded iron utensils including cooking pots of all sizes. It is believed that the utensils made in this village have a historical and sacred significance as they were used by the gurus in their langar or community meals. Even today these families receive orders from all over the state and abroad for cooking pots for community langars.

Village demography and its sacred geography

Gehuan is predominantly a Jatt Sikh village (roughly 60 per cent), followed by Hindus (15 per cent), Ravidassias (15 per cent), Valmikis (10 per cent) and a cluster of a few Muslim families. Sikh lohars (categorized under backward castes) constitute a microscopic minority. Jatt Sikhs are landed gentry, monopolizing over 80 per cent of the land, a profile that is in consonance with their state-level profile.[1] The village has the following big and small sacred sites:

1. Village-level deity: 1 (Baba Nagarkheda)
2. Temples: 7
3. Gurudwaras: 6
4. Ravidassia Gurudwara: 1
5. Valmiki temples: 2
6. Baba Farid-Sheetla Mata Temple: 1
7. Pir *mazaar*, samadhi: 1
8. Mosque: 1
9. Sati asthal: 2
10. Baba Jodh Samadhi: 1

To get a holistic sense of the complexity of the sacred geography of Gehuan, let's briefly examine what each of these sites represents.

Baba Nagarkheda

Baba Nagarkheda is a village deity, and hence is not affiliated to any particular community. It is said that when the village was founded, the people first created this brick, mud and stone structure for the safety and security of its inhabitants and for the well-being of their land and cattle. An annual fair is organized sometime in May or June to propitiate the deity and seek his divine blessings for the entire village. All the communities in the village contribute towards the organization of this annual event. Before any important event in a family, the villagers, across faiths and caste, first pay obeisance to Baba Nagarkheda. During the annual fair, the villagers collectively organize langar. Nagarkheda represents the collective solidarity of the village.

Courtesy: Author

Baba Nagarkheda Shrine

The marble tiles on the gate and the inner walls of the temple depicting Hindu and Sikh religious symbols, however, are perhaps later additions and exhibit the stamp of local power dynamics and domination. Ideally, the village deity is a secular symbol, which only recognizes the identity of a villager. But these additions also remind us how the sacred geography is used as a site of symbolic expressions of the contestations and power that characterize the world outside. The absence of symbols from other religious traditions reflects the unequal world.

Temples

Courtesy: Author

The pond of the Pandavas adjoining the Shiva temple of Gehuan

The village has a huge pond at its entry point, which is believed to have been built by the Pandavas when they were in exile. This pond has seven temples built around it. Of these, the Shiva temple, on the eastern edge of the pond, is the biggest and most frequented by devotees, not all of whom are Hindus. In the holy month of *shraavan* (July/August), when the *kaanwar* (a decorated palanquin that carries holy water and other offerings) yatra is organized to the Naina Devi shrine in neighbouring Himachal Pradesh, the entire village participates by donating money and grains for organizing langar at the shrine. People across faiths join the procession to the Naina Devi shrine, a popular Hindu pilgrimage of the region. In the Shiva temple, especially on a Monday or Saturday, it is commonplace to see turbaned men offering water and milk to the main deity and lighting a lamp at the adjoining Shani temple (dedicated to the deity of the planet Saturn).

The local priest informed me that on Saturdays, a large number of people from other faiths visit the Shani temple as the deity commands a big following. It is believed that earning his blessings ensures security of all kinds. Since the deity is a very volatile one, everyone fears his anger, and he is given special treatment by lighting earthen lamps filled with mustard oil and placing offerings of black lentils around his idol.

There are a few other small temples in the village built by business families that are recognized by the caste/family group responsible for their upkeep.

Gurudwaras

Gehuan has about half a dozen magnificent gurudwaras. It is believed that Guru Har Rai, the seventh guru, first visited the village and blessed the place. Later, the ninth guru, Guru Tegh Bahadur, came to this village, where the Akalgarh Sahib Gurudwara stands today beside a pond that is believed to have the divine power to cure all sorts of skin and other ailments. The structures reflect the material affluence and general dominance of the Jatt Sikhs in the village. Old-timers recount that these gurudwaras were smaller and humbler earlier, but with the growing prosperity of the community thanks to urbanization, and the rising value of the land due to its proximity to the city, they have made huge strides, which is reflected in the structures of the places of worship. Akalgarh Sahib Gurudwara runs a round-the-clock langar, and huge portraits of the Sikh gurus and other panthic heroes are displayed on the walls of the langar hall.

Ravidassia gurudwara

The gurudwara, exclusively for the Ravidassia community, stands as a paradox. Ravidassias, the erstwhile untouchable community, and now under the constitutional category of Scheduled Castes, though Sikhs, were never really accepted as equals by the dominant Jatt Sikhs in practice. Caste-like formations exist even among the Sikhs, and discriminatory practices at sites of worship and cremation led to the phenomenon of separate gurudwaras and funeral sites in the villages of Punjab. The mushrooming of deras of all denominations across Punjab reflects the weakening of syncretism and coexistence.[2] Caste continues to remain relevant in the socio-cultural geography of the Punjab, especially in its villages.

In Gehuan, though there is no overt display of acrimony among the communities, inter-community relations carry a muted but clear caste stamp. In ordinary conversation, people will say, 'No, there is no distinction, we are the same and we visit each other's places of worship, there is no restriction.' Yet, the very fact of the existence of a separate gurudwara for the Ravidassia community in the village challenges the claims of coexistence and mutuality.

Elderly Ravidassias recount that the gurudwara was earlier very small, and it is only recently that it has become so large. The gurudwara is looked after by a Ravidassia Granthi. Compared to the other gurudwaras in the village, the Ravidassia Gurudwara has a humble feel to it. It stands at the corner of a dingy lane, close to the part of the village inhabited by the lower castes. The gurudwara follows the Sikh *rahit maryada* (code of conduct for religious places) as no picture of Sant Ravidas can be seen anywhere—the code prohibits image worship and the conception of a guru other than the ten gurus of the Sikhs. The holy book, the Guru Granth Sahib, is the living guru for the believers of Sikhism. This is in contrast to many Ravidassia gurudwaras in the Doaba region, especially Jalandhar and its vicinity, where pictures and posters of Ravidas, Ambedkar and others often adorn the walls of the premises.

I am a Ravidassia, how can I be a kisaan?

It is clear that the chasm between the Jatts and the Ravidassias is not as tangible here as in other parts of Punjab such as the Doaba. The marginalization of the Ravidassias in the village agrarian economy in terms of land ownership is near complete. Most of them work in nearby towns and cities as craftsmen. The entry of Bihari migrants has pushed them further out of the local agriculture-based economic arrangement. The village *jamindaars*—another name for the local landed community of Jatts—now almost entirely depend on these migrant workers for their agricultural work.

During one of our field visits, a middle-aged man came and sat next to us. He was sweating heavily and his hands were muddied, so I asked him, 'Were you working in the field, are you a *kisaan* (farmer)?'

In a stern voice he replied, 'How can I be a kisaan, I am a Ravidassia.'

The comment summarized the asymmetry of the centuries-old material history of Punjab, especially of its land relations. It is in these fleeting moments that one feels and experiences the hidden text of the otherwise tranquil-looking surface of Gehuan, which then informs inter-religious community relations as well. The Gehuan Ravidassia Gurudwara has only one big poster outside where, besides the ten gurus, the *bhagats*,[3] including Ravidas, are portrayed. What is interesting, however, is that pictures of Ravidas are prominently placed in many other local and personal spaces, such as community halls and homes. The community hall near the gurudwara has a small sacred site that has pictures of many Hindu gods and goddesses, besides Ravidas. Similarly, in some of the *pakka* houses in the Ravidassia locality, one can see pictures of Ravidas and other Hindu deities printed on tiles and displayed prominently. These instances indicate a propensity to fuzziness and reflect the ambiguity or tentativeness in the domain of the sacred among the Ravidassias.

Pir Mazaar

Gehuan has a samadhi or pir mazaar (shrine), as they call it. The family that looks after it, and who had it constructed within the premises of their house, belongs to the Sikh lohar community. It is said that the family initially met with a series of unfortunate accidents and economic misery, and it was then that one of the elders had a dream that the house was built on a pir mazaar. He was advised that if the family wished to end its misfortunes, they must resurrect the samadhi and worship it. They did exactly that, and it is believed that since then there have been no mishaps in the family. A portion of the house, painted a deep olive green, has been exclusively set aside for the samadhi, and the various rituals, such as lighting the lamp, are performed by the family members. A mix of Hindu and Islamic symbols are placed near the shrine, such as a trishul, chimta and other items associated with fakirs and sadhus, creating an evocative maze of syncretism.

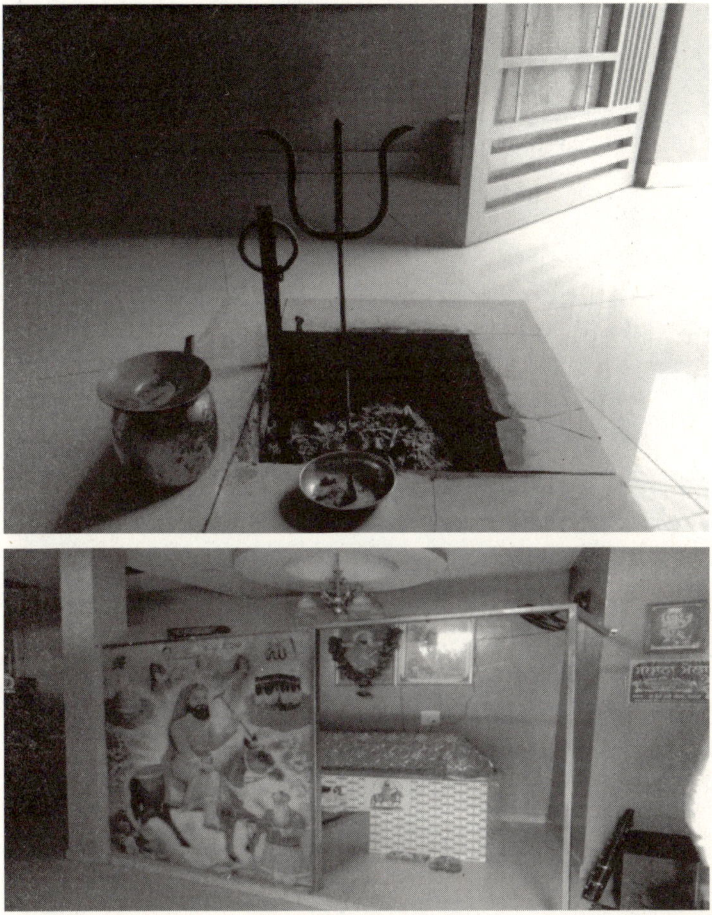

Courtesy: Author

Pir Mazaar of Gehuan

Valmiki temple

The Valmiki community resides close to the Ravidassias of Gehuan. They are numerically larger only than the Muslims, the most marginal segment, with just a few households in the village. The Valmiki temple represents another end of the religious spectrum of Gehuan, characterized by a

Courtesy: Author

The Village Valmiki Temple

mind-boggling fuzziness of religious and faith boundaries. The newly renovated temple has pictures and paintings of Valmiki, Ganesh, Ram-Lakshman, Durga, Banda Bahadur, Guru Govind Singh, and many other dieties and saints drawn from multiple sources, but largely from Hinduism. There is a statue of Sant Valmiki holding the Ramayana, the holy book authored by him, in the sanctum sanctorum, while the surrounding walls are covered with images and paintings of gods and goddesses, depicting legends from varied traditions.

Baba Farid-Sheetala Mata Temple

Courtesy: Author

Baba Farid-Sheetala Mandir

Close to the Valmiki temple is another sacred site, which has two large paintings, one of Baba Farid, located in one corner, and another of Mata Sheetala, in another corner. The sanctum sanctorum is occupied by Mata Sheetala, and the deity is surrounded by pictures of Baba Farid, Baba Gorakh Nath and Baba Balak Nath, traditions that have their roots in the country's north-western regions. At the entry of the temple is a small area dedicated to the Sheetla Mata *jyot*, or flame, where earthen lamps are lit by devotees. When I visited, a motley group of people, mostly youth, were sitting on a mat on the floor in the space outside the sanctum sanctorum. They were all from the Valmiki community, including the priest of the shrine, Sant Sukhveer Singh, who looks after the temple. An old man, probably about seventy, recounted, on being asked about the antiquity of the temple, 'I do remember its existence for as far back as I can remember, since my childhood. Though earlier it was not as decorated and organized and big as it is now, but it existed always.' None, however, could explain the shrine's historical legacy and the merging of the tradition of Baba Farid, a Sufi saint, with the folklore of Sheetala Mata, believed to be one of the forms of Goddess Durga, the goddess of *shakti* (divine force) in the Hindu pantheon.

Sati asthal

The village has two sati asthals, sites commemorating the tradition of sati. They are exclusively family-based sacred places. The families, from the Hindu community, have continued the tradition as it was followed by their forefathers. These sites are usually constructed by the respective families on their private land. They typically comprise a concrete structure covered with a red cloth or *chunri*, denoting Goddess

Sati. The family organizes an annual langar and puja, and the daily upkeep is the responsibility of the family. A member of a family that has a sati asthal informed me, 'Our ancestors were probably from the Rajasthan region where the practice of sati was prevalent, maybe the tradition has continued since then. But of course, no one practices that tradition anymore. We revere it, as it is to do with our ancestors, and it is believed that by worshipping the deity, we seek her blessings for our family.'

Baba Jodh Samadhi

This is a shrine dedicated to ensuring the safety of milch animals. According to legend, during the Mughal period, when Baba Jodh had taken his cattle for grazing in the nearby forest, one of his buffalos was killed by a Mughal official. Baba took on the assailant but could not save the buffalo. Later, a samadhi was built on the spot where the buffalo had fallen.

Mosque

The village has just one mosque, located on the outskirts. There are not more than ten or twelve Muslim households, and their numerical marginalization is reflected in their low status in the village. Most of them are craftsmen—masons, carpenters, weavers and such. The younger men are now also equipped with new skills, such as those of an electrician or a plumber, mostly in response to urban demands in the vicinity. A water cooler on the premises of the mosque, donated by a Sikh businessman from the village, reflects the general sense of coexistence and mutual respect for each other. Muslims,

I was told, also participate in the annual festival of Baba Nagarkheda, and they too, like other villagers, consider it auspicious to invoke the village deity before undertaking any new activity, such as opening a shop or initiating a marriage proposal.

What is striking about this village is the shared sense of history and the almost unconscious propensity of the people, cutting across faiths, to own its Hindu past. The legend about Gehuan's association with the Pandavas through its pond is invariably the first thing cited when introducing the village. This seamless narration of a mythical past is the bedrock of what I have referred to elsewhere as the culture of syncretic diversity[4] in this part of the world, unlike the sensibility of religious diversity in the West, which carries a sense of rigid boundaries, where religions, even in a pluralist framework, stand next to each other as insulated islands.

A grocery shop near the Nagarkheda shrine sells calendars of various gods and goddesses and images from other traditions. A glance at the calendars bears testimony to the village's ethos of coexistence. Apart from images of Mecca and Madina, Baba Farid, the Sikh gurus, Baba Gorakh Nath, Baba Balak Nath and Baba Johar Peer, the presence of Macchliwaale Baba was quite amusing. This list exhibits the core values of syncretism and the inclusive religious cosmos. Machchliwaale Baba turned out to be a cult of Jhule Laal, of Sindhi origin. Despite the fact that there is not a single Sindhi family in the village, the presence of this cult indicates the sturdiness of the syncretic grid of diversity and pluralism. The ancestral connection with the folklore from the region, it is clear, has remained despite the land undergoing a painful partition and reorganization of territory at the cost of human memory, life and history.

Courtesy: Author

Calendars collected from a shop near the Baba Nagarkheda shrine at Gehuan

Courtesy: Author

Vishwakarma's pictures on the walls of an ironsmith's workshop

Likewise, among the Sikh lohar community, the walls of their small factory shops tell the story of a historically pluralistic religious milieu. Among the calendars and framed pictures of various Sikh gurus, one will invariably find a picture of the legendary Vishwakarma, the Hindu god considered to be the main deity of craftsmen, especially those dealing with ironwork such as making *kanda*, or the cooking pot, as discussed above. A confused, even amused, response to the question, 'Why Vishwakarma, when you are a Sikh?' by the respondents from the community indicated how naturally multiple identities coalesce in these cases, and any interrogation of this 'naturalness' only invites an expression of dismissiveness of the questioner's lack of knowledge about something so obvious and commonly shared in this part of the world.

Messages

The village, despite exhibiting a peaceful attitude towards its multiplicity of faiths, clearly bears the imprint of caste in its everyday life. As one villager shared, 'If there are three Kuldeeps in the village, they will be known as Kuldeep 1, Kuldeep 2, Kuldeep 3, depending on the person's caste location.' This response from a member of the Valmiki community highlights the prevailing caste hierarchy in the village. The interesting thing revealed by the Gehuan experience is the relationship between religion and caste and how the fuzziness of boundaries changes as one moves up the hierarchy—it actually decreases as one moves towards the top. In other words, the higher the dominance and caste rank, the lower the level of fuzziness. Hindu temples and Sikh gurudwaras will follow their broad scriptural prescriptions and demonstrate an autonomous universe where the emphasis is on the singularity of their own postulates. In contrast, among the Ravidassia and Valmiki, the places of worship show ample signs of a propensity for diversity and coexistence.

In Gehuan, the most diversity-friendly shrine or religious place was that of the Valmikis. How does one explain or understand this inverse relationship between caste location and fuzziness of religious boundaries among the various groups of Gehuan? One line of argument could be that once a group or community in a caste framework achieves a certain level of economic prosperity and local social dominance, it then tends to claim and announce its position or status by segregating and emphasizing its separate history. On the other hand, the Valmikis of Gehuan appear to be the repository of the old world charm of Gehuan. For instance, the Baba Farid-Sheetala Mata Mandir is managed and maintained by the Valmikis, which establishes their inclination to foster diversity rather than promote any single framework of faith. It is important to remember that Baba Farid is one of the prominent bhagats whose verses have been incorporated in the Guru Granth Sahib, the holy book of the Sikhs, and hence he is a revered figure in the local cultural context.

This fusion of varied traditions—from Sikhism, Hinduism and Islam/Sufism—resonates with Gehuan's broad and traditional old world. Syncretism has been the hallmark of Sikhism—it has borrowed from contemporary sant traditions across all strata and faiths. This tradition is quintessential to gurudwaras all over the world. However, the caste factor has diluted its scriptural claim of a non-hierarchical world.[5] The possibility of a religious place named after Baba Farid and Sheetala Mata is an extraordinary one, and the location of such a space among the Valmikis of Gehuan only corroborates the argument about the relation between caste location and diversity. Even among the Ravidassia of Gehuan, though their gurudwara reflects the singularity of Sikh rahit, many other structures in the vicinity show a tendency similar to that of the Valmikis to embrace other faiths. A religious structure near the Ravidassia community hall has figures of Ravidas, Lord Shiva, Lakshmi and many other gods and goddesses, including pictures of Baba Johar and Baba Balak Nath.

It is noteworthy, however, that this largely pluralistic and syncretic social fabric of Gehuan is currently undergoing transformations in the face of large-scale changes happening in the vicinity. The village's proximity to Chandigarh and the increased pressure on it from the real estate industry have brought in new institutions and structures. Recently, a huge campus of a private university has been established there, triggering significant changes, including the entry of outsiders, and massive conversion of agricultural land into commercial spaces like small cafés and hotels. A good number of young and old people from the village, and also some women, have been offered subsidiary jobs in the university. Because of these developments, the villagers have new opportunities, such as providing rented accommodation to students and others. All this seems to have impacted village life in a substantial way. Additionally, there is a massive influx of mobile-enabled information, leading to changes in the behaviour of the youth and a consolidation of caste- and community-based identity, in contrast to the collective village identity that was qualitatively more cohesive and integrated earlier. The intense free flow of messages and information has connected the village to larger networks. This has resulted in the questions and politics of identity becoming accentuated. Gehuan's sacred context also highlights the hidden text of local power dynamics, which is a function of a mix of demographic strength, material stake and caste location. The appearance of some and the invisibility of other symbols and signs in a neutral space like the Baba Nagarkheda shrine at Gehuan bear testimony to that.

The socio-cultural setting of Punjab has predominantly been coexistential. Most villages have multiple faiths and castes that are organically interwoven, with all their individual peculiarities and specificities, creating a cultural matrix that celebrates pluralism and diversity. As a border society, Punjab has had a long history of exposure to diverse ethnic, cultural and religious encounters, and therefore exchanges. Over centuries, the society has undergone transformations, like elsewhere, but the imprint of the past still shows remarkable indelibility. With increased pressures from the forces of modernity and its political economy, the cultural constituents of Punjab's society seem to be under duress, grappling with the pull of the past and the exigencies of the present. My experience, while highlighting the perseverance and robustness of the old, also brought to light the contemporary complexities that are emerging from this moment of rapid change, as experienced in this village in Punjab. Moreover, at a conceptual level, my observation was that the discussion around the idea of religion and diversity in the South Asian context, vis-à-vis the Western formulations relating to these categories, underlined the former's propensity to coalesce and coexist without following any neat compartmentalization.

As a society, Punjab has been a crucible of a multitude of ideas, traditions and world views. As writer and chronicler Khushwant Singh sums up: 'The Punjab, being the gateway into India, was fated to be the perpetual field of battle and the first home of all the conquerors. Few invaders, if any, brought wives with them, and most of those who settled in their conquered domains acquired local women. Thus the blood of many conquering races came to mingle, and many languages—Arabic, Persian, Pushto, and Turkish—came to be spoken in the land. Thus, too was the animism of the aboriginal subjected to the Vedantic, Jain, and the Budddhist religions of the Aryans, and to the Islamic faith of the Arabs, Turks, Mongols, Persians, and Afghans. Out of this mixture of blood and speech were born the Punjabi people and their language. There also grew a sense of expectancy that out of the many faiths of their ancestors would be born a new faith for the people of the Punjab.'[6]

The churning that took place amidst the tumult of material contests, it appears, spawned some powerful philosophical traditions and world views in this region. Sikhism is one such tradition. Alongside it, many other traditions prospered and were altered and reoriented in the company of each other, such as Hinduism, the Arya Samaj, Islam, Christianity, Sufism, Nath Panth, Udasis, Kabirpanthis, Valmikis and many others.

The sacred geography of Gehuan reflects the characteristics of South Asian religious traditions and their propensity to mix and merge while still retaining their individualities. Gehuan's public spaces—religious or otherwise—resonate with the spirit of togetherness, at least visibly, undermining caste and religious distinctions. But this is a cultural legacy that needs constant reaffirmation and nurturance. If preserved, it can be an exemplar for a world currently reeling under bigotry, fundamentalism and fanaticism.

The world of Gehuan still comes across as an ideal space despite the visible signs of reorientation and revision in its religious template. That a Hindu or a Sikh family worships at and maintains an overtly Islamic tradition, a mazaar, that too in the close proximity of their own residential space, and that a Muslim man offers obeisance at the Nagarkheda shrine like everyone else speaks volumes of the level of inter-faith bonding and trust.

Sadly, however, the influx of migrants and the ever-spreading corporate networks and markets have threatened to reconfigure Gehua's syncretic culture and inter-faith camaraderie. The ubiquitous mobile networks have added to the complexity of the situation through the message industry, which has unleashed the floodgates of fake narratives, accentuating the politics of identity and thereby creating doubts and insecurities. As an elderly Sikh man explained,

'Young people these days are too occupied with mobile phones and they form opinions based on information that they receive on social media through unverified sources with total disregard for our local history of harmony and peaceful existence.'

This trip to Gehuan is a fitting precursor to our main journey into the dense forest of the world of deras in Punjab. The emergence of the complex and conflict-ridden dera phenomenon in the north-west region symbolizes the troubled waters of the once tranquil and peaceful *sarovar* (lake) of Punjab. Deras have increasingly become signposts of identity politics based on caste. The promises that the mainstream and dominant traditions could not fulfil led to the mushrooming of these counter-philosophies and arguments. The underclass of the caste system waited for centuries after moving to the promised land of castelessness, but that anticipation of an equal world never came to fruition. Gradually, politics took over, and deras of all shades and persuasions prospered in the region. The mapping of Gehuan's religious landscape provides us with a starting point and works as a guide as we navigate the complex labyrinth of dera culture and politics, examining how the identities of communities, once intertwined, have struggled and grappled with each other to create their own individual worlds.

2

Deras and Caste in Punjab

Deras, as religious spaces, are popular sites among the people of the north-western region of India, including Punjab, Haryana and Himachal Pradesh. The word 'dera' essentially means a sacred place where a guru or a spiritual person either lived, is living or has some association with. The place thus becomes significant and occupies a revered status as it commemorates the memory of that sacred being and his or her connection with the particular location. The key idea is the association of the place with a sant or guru in human form.

Deras are variously referred to as 'ashrams' and 'dharamshalas' elsewhere, but the word 'dera' has far greater currency in Punjab and its adjoining states. In fact, the idea of the dera is perhaps as ancient as the existence of various religious traditions themselves. Unfortunately, in recent times, the word has become synonymous with contestation and controversy, largely because of a few deras and their unscrupulous ways.

The important point is that historically, there is nothing inherently suspicious about the dera, nor does it represent anything pathological. Rather, deras exist in the true spirit of argumentation and the culture of philosophical contestation that are so intrinsic to the religious landscape of Indic traditions. In fact, there is a town in Punjab known as Dera Baba Nanak in Gurdaspur district. It is a historical town, and some of the lanes and houses there have been preserved since the time of Guru Nanak, the first guru and founder of Sikhism. Another important aspect of the town is that from it, pilgrims can see across the border into Pakistan and have darshan of the Gurudwara Durbar Sahib at Kartarpur in Pakistan, which was built in commemoration of Guru Nanak. The place is a reminder that while territorial boundaries may have been created between the two countries, the flow of religious streams remained uninterrupted, defying the temporality of barriers.

Theoretically, therefore, deras can be defined as places or centres of religious congregation, organized mostly around a revered person and generally oriented towards community service and social welfare activities, with an emphasis on *sadachaar* or the good deeds of its believers.

In the Punjab region, the followers of a dera are led by the commands of the spiritual guru, who may or may not subscribe to the tenets of Sikhism or may even have evolved their own syncretic philosophy and codes. By one estimate, reported in 2007, there are more than 9000 Sikh as well as non-Sikh deras in the 12,000 villages of Punjab.[1] This shows the vast and complex nature of the religious landscape, which is covered with the strands of many faiths interwoven into a cohesive web.

It would not be an exaggeration to say that India's religious map has very few straight lines, as the sacred geography is inherently culturally circuitous. It would be an audacious attempt to try and find a singular line untouched by anything external and with a verticality of its own. The picture that one's mind conjures up, imagining this landscape, is of a huge and ancient banyan tree whose roots have turned into numerous trunks, almost as robust as the main tree, creating a multi-trunk tree.

It is this meshing of faiths that makes India's religious milieu complex and yet very promising. It is this sense of syncretic mutuality and trans-cultural borrowing that characterizes the Indian religious terrain.

The neatness of the religious diversity template that recognizes boundary and autonomy as its core themes tends to be a misfit when applied in the South Asian context. Hence, India's religious diversity can better be termed as 'syncretic diversity'. The template of syncretic diversity, one would argue, tends to complement and nurture the organic roots of the diverse traditions that encourage coexistence without undermining each other.

This, however, now seems to be a prototype imagination, as the format is under duress and has also undergone transformation owing to the identity politics prevalent not just locally but also globally.

In Punjab, where the dominant religious tradition is Sikhism, the trajectory that the tradition has taken bears testimony to this syncretic diversity. The history of Punjab is characterized by enormous diversity and the criss-crossing of religious traditions. Founded by Guru Nanak Dev (1469–1539), Sikhism emerged in the fifteenth century as an alternative and as a critique of the existing culture of caste and its rigid hierarchical principles of social organization. The new tradition emphasized this world and the household, contrary to the largely otherworldly orientation of Hinduism.

However, an internal ideological churning, so true to the essence of the Indic tradition, continued from the very beginning of Sikhism. Guru Nanak's own son, Sri Chand

Maharaj (1493–1643), disagreed with him. Shri Chand Maharaj, also known as Baba Shri Chand, the elder son of Guru Nanak, is considered to be the founder of the ascetic sect called Udasis, literally meaning stoic, detached or indifferent, which believed in an austere life and extolled the virtues of asceticism and other-worldliness. Popular iconography portrays Baba Sri Chand Maharaj as very similar to the Hindu god Shiva with matted hair and sitting in a meditative posture on a tiger skin.

Many consider his actions as rebellious towards his father. However, there is ample historical evidence to suggest the critical role played by the Udasis in safeguarding the Sikh tradition and history and their reverence for the Guru Granth Sahib. There were, however, differences in their world views as far as their larger philosophies were concerned. Broadly speaking, Udasis were other-worldly and renunciatory in orientation in contrast to Guru Nanak's world view.

Sikhism had a tradition of living gurus, one succeeding the other, until Guru Gobind Singh (1666–1708), the tenth guru, declared the end of this tradition. The tenth guru announced that henceforth the Guru Granth Sahib, the holy book, would be the guru.

During the period when the tradition of a living guru continued, the transition was not always smooth. As a result, various deras of Minas, Udasis, Dhirmalias, Ram Raiyas, Masandis and others mushroomed. All these groups primarily emerged due to the disgruntled claimants to gurudom. Many more deras emerged at various points in time during the consolidation of the Sikh religion.

Historically, the following are the ten living gurus of Sikhism: Guru Nanak (1469–1539), Guru Angad (1504–1552) Guru Amar Das (1479–1574), Guru Ramdas (1534–1581), Guru

Arjan Dev (1563–1606), Guru Hargobind (1595–1644), Guru Har Rai (1630–1661), Guru Harkrishan (1656–1664), Guru Tegh Bahadur (1621–1675) and Guru Gobind Singh (1666–1708).

The tenth guru essentially gave Sikhism a formal structure and symbol orientation, leading to a distinct identity. The *panth* (community) from here on moved from its broadly eclectic and fluid orientation to a more neatly defined identity. Guru Gobind Singh declared the Khalsa (pure) with the inauguration of the five Ks, namely, kesh (uncut hair), kara (a steel bracelet), kangha (a wooden comb), kirpan (steel sword) and kachcha (cotton underwear).

However, despite these symbols, the process of creating a neat demarcation and boundary that would insulate the community from others continued to elude complete closure. This is reflected in many forms, such as the persistence of the Keshdhari, Amritdhari, Sehajdhari, Nirankari, Namdhari, Neeldhari and many other identities. Though all of them follow Sikh rahit maryada and consider themselves Sikhs, there are deviations of various grades from what is considered by the organizers of the panth as the 'core'.

Those who have been baptised by the ceremony of taking the amrit and embrace the five Ks, pay *dasvandh* (spending one-tenth of their earnings on philanthropy and sacred work) and follow the code of conduct as prescribed are the Khalsa Sikhs and are considered the 'purest'.

Who is a Sikh and who is not? This question remains a matter of debate within and between the community and panthic bodies like the Shri Gurudwara Prabandhak Committee (SGPC), responsible for the management of the gurudwaras and Sikh places of worship in the states of Punjab and Himachal and the Union Territory of Chandigarh.

Every now and then, the question takes centre stage, giving rise to intense debates before the matter subsides, though the questions linger on.

Indian, or rather South Asian, social history and its ecosystem have an organic, lukewarm response to the idea of religion with a neat boundary, rarely viewing it as a 'bounded' community with a clear sense of membership and non-membership. New ideas, philosophies and world views continue to prosper and mushroom in proximity to each other. There is a certain element of defiance inbuilt in the Indic traditions towards the rigid template of religion.

A fluid framework that encourages porous boundaries characterizes the sacred landscape of India. This is also amply evident, for instance, in the complex nature of the debates on religious conversion in India. The incompleteness and doggedly unfinished nature of conversion is reflective of the porosity and elasticity of religious boundaries. In other words, even though people and groups might have converted, their connection with the past and its broader normative universe remains alive and refuses to disappear. The enmeshment of caste and religion plays a significant role here.

The idea of a living guru and caste

In the mushrooming of deras in contemporary times, and even in the past in north-west India, two factors are critical: contestations over the idea of a living guru and the concept of caste. Although the tenth guru declared that Sikhism would no longer follow the tradition of a living guru and proclaimed that the Guru Granth Sahib or *Bír* would henceforth be treated as the guru, the associated cultural environment did not change as easily. New claimants to gurudom with alternative philosophies flourished simultaneously, some overtly and many others in a subdued manner.

This then became a major point of disagreement and contestation as the conservative elements viewed those disagreeing or diverting from the established or embedded as violating the maryada of Sikhism. The important point is that given the shared roots, it has been common in the region to find people from other faiths also revering the Guru Granth Sahib. In such a context, places of worship that continued to abide by their age-old reverence for the Guru Granth Sahib but also came to be organized under a living human guru naturally became flashpoints, and the relationship became strained.

For example, even within Sikhism, those who experimented with the core template, like the Nirankaris and Namdharis, became, in some form, deviants. Many term these sects as Sikh deras as they are organized under a living guru-like figure but follow other Sikh rahits and maryada. There were many others who, though they continued to revere the Guru Granth Sahib, did not necessarily conduct their affairs within the framework of Sikh maryada. Such places of worship were referred to by many as non-Sikh deras.

The moot point is the tussle between conservative elements and those whose world views have been influenced and shaped by the dynamics of the contemporary and the present. The latter naturally show a propensity for experimentation and new additions. With the entry of caste, another layer or frame of contestation was added.

Theoretically, Sikhism has always espoused an egalitarian world and has, in fact, been a major counter-philosophy to the caste-ridden social order in which it germinated and took shape as a new faith. Institutions such as *sangat* (non-hierarchical congregation), langar (community partaking of food), *pangat* (inter-community dining irrespective of caste and creed) and *Panj Pyare* (initiated by the tenth guru as the chosen favourite disciples from all strata), portray its core philosophy, which counters the logic and grammar of caste. In this sense, Sikhism emerged as a major egalitarian rebuttal to a caste-ridden society. Furthermore, the verses and hymns contained in the Guru Granth Sahib are a commentary on the panth's foundational assertion of inclusivity and equality.

The Guru Granth Sahib contains verses and hymns from a host of sants, coming from varied caste-religious milieus, many of them with lower caste backgrounds, such as Kabir, Ravidas and others (all of whom lived in the fourteenth and fifteenth centuries). The Guru Granth Sahib contains 224 hymns and 237 shlokas of Kabir and forty hymns of Ravidas.[2] This reflects the inclusive, syncretic philosophy of the Sikh gurus, for whom the eradication of this-worldly injustices remained a paramount concern over other-worldly anxieties.

Expectedly, the new tradition received an enthusiastic reception from those at the base of the caste pyramid. While the Jatt Sikhs, largely from the agrarian and landed community, were the early entrants who thronged the new panth as its earthy philosophies suited their existential world, the lower castes from the Hindu fold were not far behind, as they too embraced the sangat in droves. However, the proverbial gap between theory and practice proved to be true here, as the theoretical claim of egalitarianism that the panth propounded so forcefully gradually gave way to caste-like formations that emerged within Sikhism in practice. As elsewhere, caste had surreptitiously entered even those spaces that emerged as its antidote.

Caste and its contextuality prosper in proximity. Caste, in that sense, is a truly relational concept; it needs a favouring ecosystem to embed itself even in an alien territory, and that it found in plenty. Over a few centuries, the Jatt Sikhs emerged as the dominant caste, monopolizing both the temporal and sacred spaces. The dominant caste status of the Jatts is a function of their numerical strength, their ownership of more than 80 per cent of the land, their being major stakeholders in Punjab's agriculture, and their historical martial status, among others.

The lower castes that had joined the panth in anticipation of an equal, dignified world found the waiting in the corridor of uncertainty almost unending. Though the Dalits of Punjab have substantial numerical clout, in terms of land ownership, they are marginalized. This forced a large number of them to be employed as agricultural labourers working on the lands of the Jatts. The unequal treatment meted out to those with a lower caste background by the Jatt Sikhs is a reality. Most gurudwaras, Sikh deras, other places of worship and even the SGPC are under the dominant control of the Jatt Sikhs.

A study done on the caste background of the members of the SGPC in 2007 found that 80 per cent of its administrative posts are held by Jatt Sikhs, 15 per cent by other castes and only 5 per cent by the Dalits.[3] Here, too, a large number of them are likely to be in the category of *sevadaars* (clerical/menial staff), and very few of them are likely to be in the positions of Granthi or *raagi* (more 'prestigious' posts in Sikh places of worship).

In other words, the imprint of caste hierarchy in Sikhism, instead of getting diluted and annihilated, became more visible and operational. The Dalits were treated as inferior in the gurudwaras, at cremation grounds and in matters of other social engagements such as marriage. Gradually, caste discrimination emerged. This disillusionment with the mainstream led to the alienation of the lower-caste groups and a progressive gravitation towards parallel religious spaces that were mushrooming with alternative philosophies or world views, often drawn from their own histories or sant traditions, such as Ravidas, Kabir or Valmiki.

Of course, this did not happen overnight. Nor is the split decisive. The religious cauldron in the region remains alive with new questions and ideas. The domination of the Jatt Sikhs over the Dalits was initially unresisted, but not for long. Decades of hard work, the consolidation of identity, the impressive presence of the diaspora, state-sponsored measures for the upliftment of the lower strata post-independence and local economic rearrangements leading to an exodus of Dalits to non-farm jobs in the cities all strengthened the materiality of the Dalit identity.

The first and perhaps most formidable subaltern expression of the caste-religion debate around a separate identity was with the Ad-Dharm movement under the leadership of Babu Mangoo Ram in the early decades of the twentieth century. Mangoo Ram, a Ghadarite, returned from California in the US to his village, Mugowal, in Hoshiarpur and fought for a separate identity for the lower castes of the region under a new canopy term called Ad-Dharm or the 'original religion', which stood apart from Hinduism or Sikhism. The movement persuaded about 5,00,000 untouchables to register as Ad-Dharmis in the 1931 Census.

However, for various reasons, the movement subsided and gradually petered out in the post-Independence period, especially after the demise of Mangoo Ram. But the term 'Ad-Dharm' remained in currency in the region and has found more vocal expression in recent times around a dera called Dera Sachkhand Ballan, located in the village of Ballan in Jalandhar district, Punjab.

The dera at Ballan, variously known as Dera Ballan or Dera Sachkhand Ballan, is a Ravidassia dera that has become the fulcrum of a new identity articulation around the teachings and philosophies of the fifteenth-century Bhakti poet, Guru Ravidas. Most Ad-Dharmis have traditionally been associated with leather work and the hide business, and Sant Ravidas also came from the same caste-occupation background. This connection led Dera Ballan to articulate the new religious identity of Ravidassia Dharm rather than Ad-Dharm in 2010.

The community, though, is divided on what should be the appropriate canopy—Ad-Dharmi or Ravidassia. There is a churning within the deras that are organized around the teachings of Ravidas. Many do not consider the Ravidassia template to be appropriate, and even other lower-caste groups, such as the Valmikis, find it exclusionary and divisive as it privileges one set of traditions over others.

Historically, there is nothing new in this development. As a result of exclusionary practices within the caste framework, a significant number of fluid religious spaces emerged, largely populated by the erstwhile lower castes and untouchables.

As the process and politics of representation picked up in the late nineteenth and early twentieth centuries, with caste and religion as the major axes, this vast swathe of fluid space became a poaching ground for the conversion wings of the mainstream religions. Hindu, Sikh, Arya Samaj, Islamic and Christian groups actively attempted to attract these marginalized groups to their denominations. This was done essentially to consolidate their numerical strength for a larger share of political power in the emerging scenario.

This is the backdrop in which deras of all hues mushroomed and flourished across the region.

3

Dera Sacha Sauda: Manufactured Halo in a 'Little Fiefdom'

Even though the landscape of northwest India, especially Punjab, is dotted with thousands of deras, there are some who keep the dera phenomenon consistently in the national and international headlines through the smouldering cauldron of controversies. Haryana's Sirsa-based Dera Sacha Sauda (DSS), under its current *gaddi nashin* or head, Gurmeet Ram Rahim Singh Insan, is one such dera.

Since 2007, when he was accused of impersonating Guru Gobind Singh—which in the Sikh maryada constitutes *beadbi* (disrespect)—Ram Rahim has been in the news for anything but sacred reasons. Currently serving a twenty-year jail term at the Sunaria Jail in Rohtak, Haryana, for crimes including rape and murder, he is able to regularly secure furlough, often before elections or other electorally significant events either in Punjab, Haryana or Rajasthan.

His twenty-day furlough in February 2022 was followed by a thirty-day one in June 2022, and another forty-day furlough in October 2022. His release from jail in the year

Courtesy: Author

Dera Sacha Sauda

2023 included a forty-day one in January, thirty days in July, twenty-one days in November. In January 2024, he was granted release for fifty days, and in August, furlough for 21 days. Most recently, in October 2024, he was released on a twenty-day parole. So, in total, the Dera sant has been out of jail for 232 days in two years.[1]

Interestingly, during these periodic releases from prison, he conducts satsangs or religious congregations and delivers lectures online, in which thousands, including public representatives and political heavyweights, participate to seek his blessings. These darshans and satsangs are organized not just to demonstrate his dominance over the empire he has created under the DSS but also to send the message that, rather than waning, his influence has grown since his conviction.

Dera Sacha Sauda's mercurial rise under Ram Rahim may be ridden with controversies, but it has been a phenomenal journey. Born into a Jatt Sikh family in Gurusar Modia village in Sri Ganganagar, Rajasthan, as Gurmeet Singh, he gradually added 'Ram', 'Rahim' and then 'Insan' (human) to his name to foster a sense of inclusivity and syncretism around the dera, which had remained relatively inconspicuous before he took over the leadership. Founded by the ascetic Beparwah Mastana from Baluchistan, who was a follower of Baba Sawan Singh, the second satguru of the Radha Soami Satsang of Beas, the dera gradually consolidated itself in Sirsa, Haryana, where it is currently headquartered.

After Baba Mastana, the gaddi of the ashram was passed on to Sant Satnam Singh. Baba Satnam Singh carried on the ascetic legacy of his predecessor, remaining out of the limelight even as the dera grew in membership and influence not just in Haryana, but also in Punjab, Himachal Pradesh and pockets of other neighbouring states. However, it was after Gurmeet Singh took over the reins of the dera that it rose to prominence and grabbed national and international attention.

There are unconfirmed versions about how the leadership of the dera passed from Sant Satnam Singh to Gurmeet Singh. While Gurmeet Singh's faction claims that Sant Satnam found Gurmeet to be a blessed and committed disciple and was hence his favourite when it came to handing over the baton, others believe that Gurmeet and his associates used force and coercion to influence the passing on of the gaddi, pressuring Sant Satnam Singh to declare Gurmeet Singh his successor.

Be that as it may, the fact remains that Gurmeet Singh took over DSS and turned it into a huge network of organizations with massive political and economic clout. It has developed into a little fiefdom in Sirsa, with a vast, independent township that includes almost everything it needs, including an elaborate security apparatus.

Located in a sprawling campus of over 700 acres, the dera headquarters is well equipped with a stadium, a 100-seater revolving restaurant, a boutique, a beauty parlour, banks, a hospital and more. Gurmeet Singh, who likes to be called *Pitaji* (father) by his followers and devotees, runs the organization like a professional venture, exhibiting amazing entrepreneurial acumen. He and his team took a keen interest in the socio-cultural milieu in and around Sirsa, planning and executing their community outreach activities accordingly.

Three activities—blood donation, drug de-addiction and mass marriages of girls and boys from poor families—stand out as testimony to this approach. All three became DSS's trademark activities, catering to the marginalized and poor families in the region. Gurmeet Singh's following grew exponentially in Punjab as well, especially in the Malwa region, which, compared to the other two regions—Doaba and Majha[2]—is the poorest pocket of the state.

The rise of the Dera Sacha Sauda in Punjab followed a similar trajectory. It attracted the poor and the Dalits from the region who were looking not only for economic patronage but also for a social shield to fight the caste discrimination they experienced at the hands of the dominant land-owning community of the region. Reeling under social, economic and political marginalization, poor people thronged to Gurmeet Singh's satsangs and congregations.

There was massive disillusionment with the state due to the slow economic revival in the post-militancy period, and the poor segments of the state, doubly hit by the agricultural slowdown and decline, were rudderless. There was rampant drug abuse and an escalation in suicides in the 'grain basket' of the nation and the land of 'agriculturists par excellence'. It was at this juncture of hopelessness and economic downturn that the DSS spread its activities in the region. The organization's claims of being a Guinness World Record holder in blood donation and running drug de-addiction camps reflect the transition that the state was undergoing and how the dera used the moment as an opportunity to establish itself.[3]

Controversy with the Sikhs

Much before the dera came into the limelight because of Gurmeet Ram Rahim Singh's criminal deeds, which led to his sentencing and imprisonment, the DSS had been at loggerheads with the Sikhs and their panthic organizations, including the

SGPC. As is well known, the Sikh religion is symbol-sensitive, and despite its historical emergence as a counter to Hinduism's elaborate rituals, it eventually also developed a code of conduct—maryada—with its related prohibitions and taboos. It is another matter that these codes and other prescriptions have been the subject of arguments and debates even within the Sikh community, and there has never been a consensus on their final form.

Even though the various segments orient themselves around the universally revered Guru Granth Sahib, there is enough space for continuing arguments and debates regarding any standardized version of a code of conduct. Most deras, both Sikh and non-Sikh, experiment and tend to deviate from the announced standard version of the code of conduct, and hence they often have a strained relationship with the Sikh panthic organizations.

A major flashpoint is the idea of a living guru. In Sikh maryada, the living guru tradition ended with Guru Gobind Singh, the tenth Guru, and henceforth the Guru Granth Sahib became the guru. Therefore, following a living guru beyond the tenth guru is a violation of the code of conduct or maryada. Most deras, including Sikh ones like Namdhari and Nirankari, who otherwise follow all the other codes, have courted controversies and even clashed with fundamentalist elements on this issue.

In the case of DSS, the flashpoint was not just the act of following a living guru but also the fact that the name of the dera was borrowed from an incident in Guru Nanak's life. It is believed that the young Guru Nanak was once given a sum of money by his father to invest in business and secure a profitable return. When his father asked him later what he had done with the money, Nanak replied that he had bought food and distributed it amongst the poor. This was what he believed to be a *sacha sauda* (true business).

The term 'sacha sauda' is, therefore, part of the sacred legends of the Sikh tradition. This supposed appropriation of a Sikh legend became a flashpoint when the DSS experimented further with innovative ideas, such as when Gurmeet Singh allegedly impersonated Guru Gobind Singh in 2007, leading to a long-drawn conflict between the DSS and the Sikhs that shows no signs of ending.

On 14 May 2007, Punjab witnessed violent clashes between the followers of DSS, known as *premis*, and Sikh groups.[4] The provocation was an advertisement in a local newspaper that showed dera chief Gurmeet Ram Rahim Singh dressed like the tenth guru, Guru Gobind Singh, administering *ruhani jam* or sacred water while inducting followers to the sect in Salabatpura, a village in the Bathinda district of Punjab. This was akin to the manner in which Guru Gobind Singh had baptized Sikhs at the time of their initiation into the Khalsa.

The dera chief's act of mimicking the sacred iconography of the tenth guru shocked the followers of the Sikh panth. Sikh organizations and other panthic groups promptly declared it an act of blasphemy, and protests and demonstrations followed all over Punjab. These soon spread to neighbouring states, with Sikh organizations demanding action against the dera chief for the sacrilege he had committed. These protests and demonstrations brought back dark memories of the days of militancy in Punjab, which had witnessed similar clashes between the Akalis and the Nirankaris.

There were reports that secessionist slogans had been raised at many protest sites, making the atmosphere ominous. The SGPC demanded the excommunication of the dera chief and the closure of all the deras as the protests intensified both locally and abroad. Later, the demand for a public apology from the dera chief for his act was raised, which was endorsed by the then Shiromani Akali Dal (SAD) government led by Prakash Singh Badal.

Interestingly, the government initially appeared reluctant to intervene as the protests spread. Political commentators and observers attributed the slow response to two factors. First, many believed the government had an axe to grind with the dera chief, as it was thought that he had backed the opposition in the previous election held in February 2007, which led to the SAD losing several seats in the Malwa region where the dera has considerable influence. Second, the government did not want to go on an overdrive to restore normalcy and be perceived by the majority community of the state as neutral at a time when the community needed their support. That would have eroded the party's traditional panthic support. In fact, one article commented, 'There is a lesson in Nero's Rome for Punjab Chief Minister Prakash Singh Badal', condemning the violence and criticizing the government for its slow and delayed response.[5]

Amid tremendous media pressure, active support and intervention from an all-party faith group, and calls from the business community to restore normalcy—for the deteriorating law and order situation had affected them the most—the dera appeared to relent. A series of apologies were issued by dera spokespersons, but none by the dera chief himself. The SGPC and the Akalis seemed less than satisfied even after the dera published a letter unequivocally apologizing for the act of imitation. The issue was that the apology had been addressed to the tenth guru, Guru Gobind Singh, in clear defiance of the panthic bodies.

This act of defiance by Gurmeet Ram Rahim Singh ensured that the truce between the DSS and the sikh panthic and other radical groups remained an uneasy one. Gurmeet Ram Rahim, who had survived physical attacks by the radical groups, was put under Z category security by the government.

The period between 2007 and 2017 was a mixed bag for the DSS and Gurmeet Ram Rahim. On the one hand, the dera's fortunes soared high as it expanded into Uttar Pradesh, Punjab, Delhi, Himachal and even abroad. On the other hand, there were ongoing court proceedings involving the dera chief in serious cases of murder and rape. The murky dealings of the Sirsa-based dera were running parallel to the rise of Gurmeet Ram Rahim as a pop singer and movie star.

His songs became a rage among his followers, especially the 'Love Charger' series, the video of which was a heady mix of boastful lyrics and visuals of the dera chief in garish attire, surrounded by a bevy of fancy imported cars, performing miraculous stunts and action sequences. These videos and songs were all about the promotion of the dera chief as a superhuman. Later, in 2015, the movie *Messenger of God* or MSG, produced and directed by the dera, was screened in various cinema halls in Punjab and Haryana. The songs of the film were written and sung by the chief himself. It was an out-and-out Gurmeet Ram Rahim Singh entrepreneurial enterprise targeted at self-glorification and brand building.

It was claimed that the movie did great business. The dera encouraged its followers to watch the film, which starred Ram Rahim in the lead role. The dera chief's persona as a social reformer who was also battling the drug mafia was portrayed prominently to synchronize his real and reel life images. Brand MSG received traction among his followers, and coupled with some smart advertorial propaganda in prominent newspapers, it appeared to be a successful venture.

While the Sirsa-based dera gradually emerged as a fiefdom lorded over by the dera chief from his elaborate fortress-like arrangement inside, the outside world, especially his followers—most of whom were from the underclass and the Dalits of the region and were seeking patronage and support—looked pretty optimistic as well. The political clout of the dera and its chief grew manifold during this period, especially in Punjab and Haryana.

Unlike the other deras, the DSS was far more open about its support for one or another political party. In Punjab, they were initially perceived to be close to the Congress, which the Akalis nurtured as a grudge when they came to power. As previously mentioned, the Akalis suffered a setback in the Malwa region in the 2007 election, where Gurmeet Singh and his dera exerted a strong influence.

What worked in favour of the dera in this area was their highly imaginative and sociologically smart outreach programmes such as drug de-addiction, blood donation and mass marriages of girls and boys from poor families, which resonated deeply with their financially impoverished clientele as these programmes addressed the challenges they faced. This coincided with the state's progressive withdrawal, beginning in the 1990s, from sectors such as education and health, leaving the poor and marginalized to fend for themselves. Naturally, they drifted towards deras, which promised them basic amenities for mere survival. The DSS then used these followers as cheap labour on dera farms and to run other projects. A large number of these followers settled in the township, and many left their sons and daughters in the service of the dera and its chief.

While many expensive infrastructural marvels within the DSS campus at Sirsa made headlines because of their architectural pomp, the one that remained shrouded in mystery and became much talked about was Ram Rahim's cave, or *gufa*, which was his abode or private space. The story of Honeypreet, the close aide and confidante of Gurmeet Ram Rahim, who was also considered his adopted daughter, as narrated by her estranged husband to the media, added to the murkiness of the dera campus and its gufa.[6]

Over the years, stories of sexual exploitation, rape, the illegal confinement and disappearance of sevadaars who did not toe the line or follow the diktats of the dera have appeared in the press. However, three cases in particular—the rape of two women devotees, the 2002 murder of Ram Chander Chhatrapati, a local journalist from Sirsa who allegedly had knowledge of Gurmeet Singh's wrongdoings and threatened to expose him, and alleged instances of forced castration—turned out to be the albatross around the dera chief's neck. He was unable to negotiate settlements in his favour despite all his political connections and economic might. These cases eventually led to his imprisonment.

Many who thought that these convictions would sound the death knell for this entrepreneurial baba's little fiefdom and his pop religiosity were, however, in for a surprise as Gurmeet Ram Rahim Singh reinvented himself through his online satsangs and darshans and by declaring Honeypreet as 'Ruhani Didi' and his second-in-command.

On 25 August 2017, Ram Rahim was convicted of rape by a special Central Bureau of Investigation court. His conviction led to large-scale violence and arson in Panchkula, Haryana, by DSS supporters, who had assembled in large numbers around the court in defiance of the public order by the police. DSS followers and strategists thought their actions would exert pressure on the court and the government and push them to reduce the severity of the chief's punishment. The violence and clashes with the police left many dead and injured. Vehicles were gutted, and there was considerable damage to public property.

None of these pressure tactics, however, worked. A couple of days later, on 28 August 2017, Ram Rahim was sentenced to twenty years in prison for raping two of his women devotees. In 2019, he was convicted of the murder of Ram Chander Chhatrapati, and in 2021 he was convicted again, along with four others, of the murder of his former manager, Ranjit Singh, also in 2002.[7]

The case relating to forced castration, filed by Hansraj Chauhan, a victim and former dera member who worked with Gurmeet Ram Rahim as a musician, alleges that the dera chief forcefully castrated hundreds of his male believers and devotees. The case is ongoing.[8]

What could be the motive of the dera chief behind this crime? Was it his insecurity or a perceived threat from some male followers that he wished to counter through this action? Or did he want a trusted but 'compromised' band of male followers who formed an inner circle around the ill-famed gufa that was mired in controversies of sexual exploits? Perhaps no one will ever know for sure, but what is certain is that the aura around Gurmeet Singh has become more sinister and murkier with these developments.

Dera under Ram Rahim: no caste, just him and his fiefdom

How does one make sense of Dera Sacha Sauda and its controversial chief, Gurmeet Ram Rahim Singh Insan? In 2013, an opportunity to attend a congregation near the Japanese Park in Rohini, Delhi, which was addressed by the chief of the DSS, was very insightful.

A large open ground had been converted into a huge venue, which was overflowing with people. An army of premis and uniformed sevadaars worked with great fervour to manage the crowd. The venue was under heavy security surveillance, from the entry gate to the inner area from where the dera chief was to deliver his sermon. The chief's personal and official bodyguards had formed a ring cordoning off the crowd. The entire area was also being monitored through CCTV. At the entry gate, each person was thoroughly frisked and checked. A large number of followers were wearing metal lockets bearing the insignia of the dera, which stated, 'God is one', and many of them had pictures of Gurmeet Ram Rahim Singh.

People—young and old, men and women—had gathered from not just Delhi and the neighbouring Haryana, but also from Punjab, Himachal, Madhya Pradesh and Rajasthan. Outside the venue were shops selling lockets, calendars, posters, herbal medicines, energy tonic, toys, albums containing photos of Gurmeet Ram Rahim Singh and CDs of his songs and videos. The common theme across all these products was the ubiquitous and exclusive presence of the dera chief. Each product carried the stamp of the dera. Nothing even remotely related to Dalit icons or history was visible. It was all about Pitaji.

There were a few images of Satnam Singh, but there was hardly anything on the founder of DSS, Beparwah Mastana Baluchistani. It appeared to be an effort to erase the not-so-dazzling past before Gurmeet Singh became Ram Rahim. The colourful guru, or Pitaji, in all his superhuman avatars was resplendent in every corner of the venue and on every product, leaving his followers spellbound and visibly star-struck. Gurmeet Singh, dressed in his trademark shiny, bright

T-shirts, hat and dark glasses, was featured on posters and calendars, depicted playing golf, driving SUVs or as a fighter. The striking imagery celebrated the alpha male image of Pitaji and depicted him as a saviour and protector.

Thousands braved the summer heat, and muscular sevadaars, men and women, tried to bring some respite by fanning themselves as they sat under the tents. Men and women were segregated.

What was unique about Pitaji's discourse was that it was a purely moral lecture, without any grand theorizing or references to philosophy or religious texts. The content revolved around how to live happily with one's family, the importance of respecting one's elders, and following healthy eating and living practices. There was no sharing of esoteric philosophical concepts dealing with questions of life and death. Gurmeet Ram Rahim Singh spoke with empathy and in a language that connected with his people, most of whom were from the underclass.

I was sitting next to a father-and-son duo. The deep attention, devotion and discipline with which they listened to the guru was remarkable and interesting. The followers were ordinary in many senses; they had all come seeking relief from health issues, childlessness and general misfortune. There was no mention of caste. No Ambedkar. No Kanshi Ram. There was nothing much on religion either.

But the bottled energy tonics and tins of protein powder with photographs of bodybuilders on their labels were in perfect consonance with the dera's profile, reflecting the chief's uncanny eye for cultural nuances and what works where. The dera understood Haryana's fascination for power sports like wrestling, and hence these products were prominently displayed.

Dera Sacha Sauda, in this sense, is a non-Dalit dera. It is an individual enterprise—an establishment of, for and by

Gurmeet Ram Rahim Singh. Yet it draws on the vast reservoir of disgruntled, free-floating individuals, overwhelmingly Dalits, who are alienated from the mainstream religious anchors in the region.

The appellations of Ram, Rahim and Insan that Gurmeet Singh has gradually added to his name point to an entrepreneurial orientation and a smart reading of the region's syncretic history. He has used these to woo this free-floating population with his flashy, jazzy ways and the creation of a space that promises his followers all the services they could ever need.

In 2016, Gurmeet Singh was conferred with an honorary doctorate by a London-based university in recognition of his record-breaking programmes in the field of social welfare like blood donation and drug de-addiction.[9] Now 'Dr' too was appended to his name, making him Dr Gurmeet Ram Rahim Singh Insan. His name was like an identity menu designed to appeal to a region that celebrated multiple and pluralistic identities.

The interesting part is that, notwithstanding his conviction in multiple cases and his imprisonment, there is no lack of zing in either the DSS or the guru's life. Rather, the dera is much more in the public eye, and its publicity networks remain as vibrant and dynamic as ever, with the guru releasing a series of videos on YouTube. During his repeated furloughs, he mostly stays in the dera campus at Barnawa, in Baghpat, Uttar Pradesh.

During the forty-day parole that was granted on 14 October 2022, he released three music videos titled *'Sadi nit Diwali'* (Every day is Diwali), *'Jaago duniya de loko'* (Awake, people of the world) and *'Chat pe chat'* (referring to mobile chatting). All three tracks were written, produced, sung and composed by him.

The Chandigarh edition of the *Indian Express* and other newspapers of 11 April 2022 were full of DSS-sponsored advertorials featuring pictures of Gurmeet Ram Rahim and the sangat. These advertorials were presented as news items. Followers of the dera celebrate April as the founding month of the Dera Sacha Sauda, as it was established by Shah Mastana Baluchistani on 28 April 1948. To commemorate and celebrate the occasion, *naam-charchas* (events involving the recitation of 'sacred words') are organized across Punjab, Himachal, Haryana and Uttar Pradesh. These events are publicized through sponsored advertorials to build the DSS brand.

The advertorials from April 2022, all similar in style and content, reported on such events from various places like Jind, Paonta Sahib, Bathinda and other centres. They highlighted three things: the guru's name—Dr Sant Gurmeet Ram Rahim Singh Insan—in bold type; the charitable works carried out by the dera, such as donating tricycles to the disabled, handing the keys of newly constructed houses to the homeless and distributing ration kits to hundreds of poor and destitute; and the dera's numerical strength of six crore followers. The campaign was unmistakably well thought out. Interestingly, that many advertorials also mentioned the date of the 'Jam-e-Insan', which was held in April 2007 and became controversial when Gurmeet Singh was accused of impersonating Guru Gobind Singh.

The strength of the DSS lies in its extensive networks of fellowship across regions, which keep the system afloat and working despite the dera being dogged by controversies. One gets the impression that this network comprises groups of trusted, long-time dera members who work as foot soldiers in the villages and towns. A central command keeps this web of networks well-oiled with funds and other amenities.

While at another time the organization and its networks may have collapsed with the chief's conviction for such heinous crimes as rape and murder, clearly this is a different time. Charisma indeed lies in the eyes of the beholder and is eternal—more so now, when there is no routinization as social media and technological tools are used to constantly reinvent the chief's mystique and make his halo shine brighter. Gurmeet Ram Rahim Singh continues to command the respect and hero-worship of his followers. His entrepreneurial acumen, coupled with his extraordinary ability to sense the direction of the political winds, has been on full display following his conviction and imprisonment.

However, there has been a change in his more recently released videos and songs, in which he appears more mellowed. A careful observation of these points towards two important shifts: one is his relatively simple and less flashy outfits as compared to his 'Love Charger' days, and the second is the focus on other sants like Satnam Singh. One of his latest videos (*Sadi nit Diwali*) shows the dera chief in the company of Satnam Singh in the earlier years, when the former was not very well known beyond the inner circle of the dera. There is also a renewed focus on issues such as drug de-addiction (*Jaago duniya de loko*) and mobile addiction among the youth (*Chat pe chat*). This is the hallmark of Ram Rahim's team—to continually focus on issues that resonate with the people in order to effectively connect with the devotee profile the organization serves.

Just when people thought the DSS was finished as Ram Rahim had been sent to jail in October 2022, the dera chief made it clear that, while for all operational purposes Honeypreet, aka Priyanka Taneja and now rechristened as Ruhani Didi, would be in charge, he would remain the dera chief.[10] That ended the debates about the future of the fiefdom that Gurmeet Ram Rahim had created through years of hard work, political manoeuvring and innovative entrepreneurship.

Yet it would be wrong to conclude that the DSS is in for a smooth run with the chief calling the shots from jail through Ruhani Didi. The controversies surrounding the DSS and the Sikhs continue to smoulder, with more accusations of beadbi by the DSS being added to the string of events and history of clashes, making the region vulnerable. The beadbi cases in 2015, where the Guru Granth Sahib was disrespected—known as the Bargari Sacrilege Cases—have been investigated, and a 2022 report by the Special Investigation Team (SIT) of the Punjab Police pins the blame on the Sirsa-based Dera Sacha Sauda and its followers.[11] The SIT mentions the disgruntled followers of the dera who were apparently upset about the non-release of the guru's film *MSG-2* in the region.

This is where the matter rests currently. Every time Ram Rahim is granted furlough in Haryana and goes to Baghpat in Uttar Pradesh, Punjab sees law and order issues cropping up. Invariably, one or the other Sikh organization protests, roads are blocked, demands are made for the repeal of the chief's furlough and questions are raised regarding the repeated 'freedom' granted to Ram Rahim. The DSS continues to thrive within the messy and perpetrually charged maze of regional politics and has managed its optics skilfully and successfully so far. But political winds are known for their mercurial nature, and the colourful saga of Baba Ram Rahim is far from over.

4

Dera Sachkhand or Dera Ballan: The Epicentre of the Ravidassia Movement

Dera Sachkhand in the village of Ballan in Jalandhar, or simply Dera Ballan, had a rather modest beginning. From a hutment in the early twentieth century, it grew to become a centre of Ravidassia identity articulation in the twenty-first century through the struggle and hard work of its sants. These sants, despite their humble background, instilled in their followers the courage to dream and the strength to be steadfast in their commitment to the cause of the community they were a part of—the Ravidassia. They belonged to a caste that was traditionally associated with leather work, which is considered polluting and thus accorded untouchable status in the social hierarchy.

Of course, the Ravidassia identity took shape much later as the dera navigated the complex caste history of Punjab, beginning with the formidable Ad-Dharmi movement led by Babu Mangoo Ram, and engaged with multiple local, national and later global political developments over its relatively short century-long history.

The problem one faces in researching and describing a localized tradition that is tucked away from the mainstream highway of knowledge production is the paucity of sources on which to build a reasonable historical narrative. For more than half a century, Dera Ballan existed in a quiet, countryside environment, away from the din and bustle of Jalandhar city. It was only towards the second half of the twentieth century that the dera began spreading it wings.

Ironically, one of the dera's projects has been, as we shall see later, to create and collect materials that illuminate its past by recognizing the heroes whom they believe have been unfairly consigned to oblivion. History-writing is a dynamic process and has always been tilted in favour of the privileged and the powers that be. Hence, Dera Ballan's quest for recording its past assumes significance.

The challenges in tracing religious histories and movements are manifold. Hagiographical accounts, oral narratives, folk utterances, travelogues, stories and anecdotes appear as lamp posts to guide a researcher stuck in the dark corridor of uncertainty.

This chapter, which draws from hagiographical accounts, based on dera sources, publications and people, is one such lamp post.[1]

Sants of Dera Ballan: the journey from Bathinda to Ballan

In the village of Gill Patti in Bathinda, Punjab, there lived a boy named Harnaam Das whose grandfather had settled in the village after moving from Joganand village near Kuttiwala (now in the Ajnala tehsil of Amritsar district) sometime in the early nineteenth century. Harnaam's parents were god-fearing and hardworking farmers. Since his childhood, Harnaam had shown a strong interest in *naam simran*, the chanting of God's name, and in nurturing trees. That he was not an ordinary child was something both his parents and neighbours sensed. He often sat in solitude under a peepal tree for hours, immersed in naam simran.

Apart from a keen interest in farming, Harnaam Das had a deep scholarly interest in Punjabi and *Amritbani*,* and he often studied themes related to renunciation and detachment. He married Bibi Shobhawanti, who was also a deeply religious lady. They had two sons, Sewa Das and Sarwan Das.

When Sarwan Das was barely five years old, his mother passed away. This made Harnaam Das disillusioned with life. Unlike his elder brother Sewa, Sarwan was spiritually inclined, a fact that Harnaam Das was aware of. One day, he decided to leave the village in quest of a higher truth. He took Sarwan with him, leaving Sewa behind to look after the farming. They wandered through towns and villages and finally decided to settle in the village of Ballan, in Jalandhar.

Harnaam Das liked the natural setting of the village and the hospitable and loving people of Ballan. After a while, Harnaam, wanderer that he was, left with Sarwan in search of another place, but soon the father and son duo started missing Ballan. Sarwan, in fact, was miserable as he missed Ballan deeply. So they returned and began living on a small patch of land on the outskirts of Ballan in a mud house given to them by the villagers. The plot had a peepal tree but it was in poor condition.

At the request of the villagers of Ballan, a sangat began to be organized for people who came to listen to Amritbani of Guru Ravidas. Harnaam Das took care of the tree, and it

* Shabads of Ravidas.

soon grew healthy. This was nothing short of a miracle for the villagers. This, it is believed, earned him the name Baba Pipal Das. Thereafter, Ballan became the *karma bhoomi* of Baba Pipal Das till he breathed his last in 1928. Throughout his life, he preached against ritualism and superstition, and advocated a simple life, respect for parents and the preservation of nature.

If Baba Pipal Das revived that small sapling and helped it stand on its own, the credit for its growth into a big peepal tree goes to his son, Sant Sarwan Das. He transformed Ballan from a collection of modest mud houses into a full-fledged dera, dedicated to spreading the teachings and baani of the fifteenth-century Bhakti sant, Guru Ravidas.

Born on 15 February 1895 in Gill Patti, Sant Sarwan Das was not just an enlightened soul; he was a dynamic and practical sant who exhorted his followers to recognize their rights and partake in a modern education while staying rooted in the cultural and historical traditions of the community. He led by example, pursued and preached his philosophy of leading a healthy life, emphasizing the merits of Ayurveda and a modern education for not just boys but also girls, while staying abreast of the political developments of the time.

While he continued with the traditions of seva, satsang and simran of his father, Baba Pipal Das, he was also a modern sant with rare vision and an unparalleled zeal for working on the ground for a bright future for his community. He was a great traveller, visiting many places and interacting with numerous people to spread the teachings of Guru Ravidas. It is said that his right foot carried the symbol of the *padam*, or lotus flower, which is a divine sign signifying an enlightened person.

Sant Sarwan Das was deeply conscious of the fact that the community that he belonged to, who traditionally worked with leather and were therefore treated as 'untouchable', needed to be made aware of their location in the social hierarchy and educated. He was an admirer of Baba Sahib Ambedkar and his philosophy.

One publication claims, 'When in 1932 Poona Pact was implemented by dint of hard work of Dr B.R. Ambedkar, the fast unto death of Babu Mangoo Ram Magowalia was discontinued by serving juice at the sacred hands of Sant Sarwan Das ji.'[2]

As documented in dera literature and publicity material, Sant Sarwan Das met Dr Ambedkar in Delhi in 1948. It was a very warm meeting, and both expressed appreciation for each other's work. This is a reflection of Sant Sarwan Das's political awareness and his empathy for the cause of the oppressed in the country. In fact, in 1970, he was instrumental in organizing a huge conference at Dera Ballan, in which 'about 20,000 people participated from Punjab, Himachal, Haryana and Jammu and Kashmir'.[3]

Apart from his interest in healthcare, education and political mobilization, he was particularly aware of the need to shape an identity for his followers, many of whom came from the lower caste community.

One of Sant Sarwan Das's dreams was to construct an impressive pilgrimage site at the birthplace of Guru Ravidas at Varanasi. He perhaps realized very early on the significance of an organizational network and base in helping the community to be recognized as equals with the 'upper castes'. The credit for the evolution and growth of Dera Sachkhand or Dera Ballan and the associated Ravidassia movement goes to Sant Sarwan Das, who remains a towering figure among the dera sant lineage, even after his death in 1972. It is not surprising, then, that the Dera Sachkhand is also known as Shri 108 Sant Sarwan Das ji Maharaj Dera.

The Dera Ballan Trust has named a large number of charitable hospitals and schools across Punjab after Sant Sarwan Das. So powerful is his legacy that even today, while there may be disgruntled voices complaining about the functioning of the dera and its current leadership, there is consensus on Sant Sarwan Das's immense contribution to the community and the Ravidassia movement.

On 11 June 1972, while attending a satsang, Sant Sarwan Das fell ill and breathed his last in a hospital in Ludhiana. On 13 June, his mortal remains were consigned to the sacred flames at Ballan in front of thousands of Dera Ballan followers. The funeral pyre was lit by two of his followers, Sant Hari Das and Sant Garib Das, who were blessed by Baba Pipal Das and who had worked closely with Sant Sarwan Das at the dera.

With the demise of Sant Sarwan Das, an era ended in the history of the Dera Sachkhand. Sant Hari Das took over the gaddi of the dera as its chief. Born in 1885 in the village of Garha, near Jalandhar, Hari Das lost his parents at a very young age. He took up the occupations of shoemaking and painting after his parents passed and worked until his sister got married.

Hari Das had been drawn to holy sants since childhood and greatly enjoyed listening to and singing kirtan. He was in search of a guru or a pious mentor who could guide him. He had heard of Dera Ballan and Baba Pipal Das, and so powerful was his urge to find a guru and get *naam daan* or *diksha*, a sort of initiation, that he followed Baba Pipal Das to wherever he addressed the sangat. He visited Dera Ballan many times to meet Baba Pipal Das. Impressed by Hari Das's devotion, Baba Pipal Das came to his village and blessed him with naam daan. Later, Hari Das became close to Sant Sarwan Das as well.

After Sant Sarwan Das had a divine dream revealing a location in Seer Goverdhanpur, Varanasi, as the birthplace of

Guru Ravidas, he entrusted Hari Das with the task of finding the spot, which was near a tamarind tree. Clearly, Sant Sarwan Das had a great deal of faith in Sant Hari Das. Indeed, the honour of laying the foundation stone at the Guru Ravidas Janam Asthan Mandir in Varanasi, which was eventually built on this site to commemorate the sant's birthplace, went to Sant Hari Das on 14 June 1965.

After the death of Baba Pipal Das, Hari Das had organized a religious congregation in his village of Garha, in which Sant Sarwan Das had participated and blessed him to free him from worldly entanglements and attachments. Sant Hari Das learnt Gurumukhi and Amritbani from Sant Sarwan Das.

Unlike his predecessor, Sant Hari Das did not pay much attention to political affairs. He was a simple soul who loved meditating in solitude, teaching children in the dera school and planting mango trees in and around Dera Ballan. His favourite engagements were to do with the satsang and naam simran. He emphasized the value of education, often saying, '*Mata shatroo, vairi pita, jo na balo pathita*', meaning, both mother and father are the enemy if they do not send their children to school. The upliftment of the community through education was a cause embraced by all the sants of the dera.

He was so inspired by Sant Sarwan Das that after the latter passed away, he had a temple with an idol of Sant Sarwan Das constructed in the dera, which was inaugurated on 11 June 1974. It was not easy to fill the shoes of a legend like Sant Sarwan Das, but Sant Hari Das as the third gaddi nashin or the chief of Dera Ballan, did remarkably well with his simple and gentle demeanour yet target-oriented leadership. Sant Hari Das passed away on 6 February 1982.

Sant Garib Das, who became the fourth gaddi nashin of the Dera Ballan, was a man of few words but with tremendous organizational skills, besides being a trained vaid or Ayurveda practitioner. Born in 1925 in the village of Jalbhey, near Adampur in Jalandhar district, Sant Garib Das not only carried forward the legacy of his predecessors and consolidated the Varanasi and Dera Ballan centres, he also took a keen interest in the aspirations of the dera's followers settled abroad.

By the early nineties, the world was witnessing a new phase of globalization, and it became increasingly easy for the global and local to engage. The new template of modernity facilitated awareness, interest and consciousness among migrants regarding their roots and the history of their ancestors. It is no wonder then that Sant Garib Das visited the United Kingdom six times, the United States thrice and Canada once during his tenure. He first visited the UK in 1985 along with Sant Ramanand, another dera follower and influential functionary who was later killed in Vienna. The foundation stone of the famous Guru Ravidas temple in Birmingham, UK, was laid and inaugurated by Sant Garib Das, as were many other guru *ghars* in both India and abroad.

His contributions included setting up the Sant Sarwan Das Charitable Hospital at Koopur-Dhypur (Kathar) in Jalandhar district, dedicated to the memory of Guru Sant Sarwan Das, on 22 October 1982; starting the weekly magazine *Begumpura Sehar*; laying the foundation stone of Sant Sarwan Das Memorial Teaching Block at Guru Ravidas Industrial Training Institute, Phagwara; building a model sarai for pilgrims in the dera; and constructing the impressive Sant Sarwan Das Memorial Gate on Jalandhar-Pathankot road.

Sant Garib Das's tenure was also known for the expansion of the dera's Varanasi project, which was now being looked after by the Shri Guru Ravidas Janam Asthan Public Charitable Trust managed by Dera Ballan. It was likely his ability to collaborate with dera sympathizers from across the political spectrum and within the administration that enabled the Janam Asthan Mandir to gain wider acceptance and recognition. No wonder that local dera detractors in Varanasi were hostile towards Sant Garib Das, as he led the project to build the Janam Asthan Mandir.

He passed away on 23 July 1994, barely a month after he had convened an impressive Dharmik Samagam at Seer Goverdhanpur in Varanasi. A large number of the attendees at this event were from overseas, and the programme also commemorated Sant Sarwan Das's death anniversary on 11 June.

On 25 July 1994, Sant Niranjan Das took over the gaddi of dera chief after the demise of Sant Garib Das. Like his immediate predecessors, Hari Das and Garib Das, Sant Niranjan Das too had the blessings of Baba Pipal Das and Sant Sarwan Das, as his parents had been disciples of the Dera Ballan sants.

Niranjan Das was born on 6 January 1942 at Ramdasspur (near Alawalpur) in Jalandhar district. His parents were regular visitors to the dera at Ballan and were close to Sant Sarwan Das. The young Niranjan Das would accompany his parents to the satsang at Dera Ballan. He earned the affection and blessings of Sant Sarwan Das during these meetings and became so close to him that he began staying at the dera when he was barely eight years old.

As the years passed by, Niranjan Das emerged as a mature and hardworking associate of the dera sants, and he took on several responsibilities related to the dera's everyday organization and events.

The involvement of the diaspora or non-resident Indians (NRIs) in the dera's organization, direction and philosophy picked up momentum during Niranjan Das's time. Along with his associate Sant Ramanand, he continued to travel overseas, visiting the UK, USA, Canada, Spain, Holland, Italy, France,

Germany, Austria, Dubai, Greece and several other countries. It is clear from this list that, unlike Sant Garib Das, who travelled to only a few countries, there was a significant expansion in the locations visited, mostly in Europe. In a way, this mirrors the pattern of overseas migration from the region: first to the UK, USA and Canada, and gradually spreading to smaller countries in Europe and even to the Gulf states.

The overseas sojourns, which were initially few and far between, picked up considerably in the mid-1990s. Punjab has been one of the few states in India whose people have had a fascination for overseas destinations, but here too the dominant Jatt community took the lead. However, the castes and communities that were socially and economically marginalized gradually joined the diaspora through sheer hard work, industriousness and a willingness to take risks. They soon prospered and now make up a reasonably affluent group in their host countries.

Sant Niranjan Das carried on the work of his predecessors, and with the generous support and growing enthusiasm of followers from overseas, the works at Dera Ballan and elsewhere, including the Janam Asthan project in Varanasi, gained momentum.

The 2009 Vienna incident and the martyrdom of Ramanand: a watershed moment

Sant Ramanand, the second-in-command of the dera chief, Sant Niranjan Das, was college-educated and a great public orator. Besides his exceptional organizational skills, he was popular for his devotional singing. He regularly accompanied the dera leaders on their overseas sojourns. His enthusiasm for Ravidas bani singing and spreading the guru's teachings to all corners of the globe was infectious, and devotees and dera followers were in awe of his selfless commitment to the cause of the community.

In April 2009, dera chief Sant Niranjan Das and Sant Ramanand embarked on a visit to Europe for about a month and a half. Italy, Germany, Greece, France, Spain, Portugal, Germany and Austria were on the itinerary. Unfortunately, this journey was cut short by an incident that eventually became a turning point in the dera's history. The two *mahants* (chief priests) reached Vienna as scheduled on 23 May. At noon on 24 May, they arrived at the Shri Guru Ravidas Temple to attend a *samagam* or congregation of their followers. The place was done up in accordance with the Sikh maryada, and the holy book, the Guru Granth Sahib, had been placed on a raised platform while the two sants sat on the floor.

However, the sacred ambience was suddenly disrupted by gunshots as some miscreants shot at the two sants. Sant Ramanand was killed, and Sant Niranjan Das was grievously injured. As news of the attack in Vienna flashed across Punjab, particularly the district of Jalandhar, followers of the dera and other Dalit bodies took to the streets, and soon Punjab was up in flames. As print and visual media broke the news of Sant Ramanand's demise and footage of the sants from the hospital they had been taken to was repeatedly shown, the crowd became hostile, plunging the entire region into a state of lawlessness.

Large-scale riots and arson followed within hours of the Vienna attack.[4] The loss of private and public property to the tune of hundreds of crores was reported in a short span of a few days. The instantaneity and scale of the violent reactions was unprecedented. Curfews were imposed in many parts of Punjab, especially in the Doaba region of the state, which is the seat of the dera and from where a large number of its followers come. Incidentally, this region is also considered the 'NRI zone' of Punjab. It is said that almost all the households here, including those of the Ravidassia community, have at least one person settled abroad. After a few days of concerted efforts from politicians, community leaders and the law and order machinery, the region showed signs of recovery.

As the reports from Vienna on the identity of the assailants who had killed Sant Ramanand filtered through the media (perceived to be Sikhs), rumour mongers had a field day. Many tried to give the incident a secessionist slant, reviving the memory of the days of militancy in Punjab. Confusing and ambivalent reports regarding the identity of those involved in the Vienna incident regularly appeared in the local newspapers, ensuring the atmosphere remained tense.

When the body of the slain Sant Ramanand was brought to the dera at Ballan, the anger that had long been smouldering within the community burst forth. It was most palpable and combative among the diaspora all over the world. News of the displacement of the Guru Granth Sahib from Ravidassia gurudwaras was reported from Italy, France and other countries.[5] Similar acts of defiance and disrespect were reported from a few places in Punjab as well. For instance, tension prevailed in a Moga village in Bhogpur, near Jalandhar, when the *bir* (holy scripture) was found on the floor and the palanquin had been replaced with a photograph of Sant Ramanand of Dera Ballan.[6]

The Vienna incident brought to the fore the simmering tension between the Ravidassia community and the mainstream Sikh tradition. While the Ravidassias followed the maryada scrupulously, the fact that they had a living guru was a bone of contention with the Sikh religious establishment. The caste angle (as discussed in Chapter 3) was also a provocation, given that the Ravidassias were considered 'lower' in the caste framework, and many at the helm of Sikh religious affairs were from the dominant castes.

The demand for a complete separation from the Sikh tradition arose from various quarters. The dera showed signs of acceeding to these demands by not organizing an *akhand path* at the *antim ardas*, or the last rites, during the funeral of the slain Sant Ramanand, in visible defiance of Sikh tradition. The movement for a separate religion picked up momentum soon after.

On 30 January 2010, on the occasion of the 633rd birth anniversary of Satguru Ravidas in Govardhanpur, Varanasi—the birthplace of Ravidas—under the leadership of the dera mahants of Ballan and in the presence of thousands of their followers and devotees, the dera declared a new religion called the Ravidassia Dharma. It had a new religious symbol with 'Hari' inscribed in the middle. The following was its charter of principles:

Our guru: Satguru Ravidas Maharaj ji
Our religion: Ravidassia
Our religious book: Amritbani Satguru Ravidas Maharaj Ji
Our salutation: Jai Gurudev
Our religious symbol: Har (i)
Our ultimate place of pilgrimage: Shri Guru Ravidas Janam Asthan Mandir Seer, Varanasi, Uttar Pradesh
Our objective: To propagate the bani and teachings of Satguru Ravidas ji. Additionally, the teachings of Maharishi Bhagwan Balmik ji, Satguru Namdev ji, Satguru Kabir ji, Satguru Trilochan ji, Satguru Sain ji and Satguru Sadna ji will also be propagated. To respect all religions, love mankind and lead a virtuous life.

In 2012, on the third anniversary of the founding of the new religion, the sacred book, Amritbani Satguru Ravidas Maharaj Ji, was introduced amidst much celebration. The dera and its sants were at the forefront of the mission to establish the new religion and its holy book. The reception on the ground, however, was lukewarm, at least among the locals around Ballan. The older generation, though aggrieved at the way the dominant tradition treated their community and the Sant Samaj, had for generations been tied to the syncretic ethos of Sikhism and a belief in the Guru Granth Sahib, and they were unhappy with such an abrupt severing of ties. The youth were angry but cautious, while the segment that appeared most aggressively in favour of a complete separation was the diaspora.

In 2013, on the occasion of the inauguration of a hospital in the name of the slain Sant Ramanand on Ravidas Jayanti, there was, as always, a strong presence of the diaspora in the newly inaugurated hospital building in village Kupur-Dhepur, Kathar, close to Dera Ballan. One individual from the UK made a passionate appeal to the large congregation, mostly local, to join the movement and become 'pakka', or 'real' Ravidassias. He appealed to them to be courageous and to not fear any dominant caste, amidst thunderous chants of '*Jo bole so Nirbhai, Sri Guru Ravidas Maharaj ki jai*' (Those who worship and chant the name of Guru Ravidas are the fearless).*

Outside the meeting hall, a conversation I had with a young local man attired in a sevadaar's uniform revealed a new perspective.† What he said was indicative of the situation at the local level: 'These people will leave after making these exhortations, and more importantly, they have the economic

* These are from author's fieldwork notes.

† Ibid.

and social clout to protect themselves. But what about us? Our life and survival depends on the local dominant groups, mostly Jatt Sikhs, and if we do not follow their dictates, we will face the backlash,' said the young Ravidassia amidst almost universal approval from those around him.

The seating arrangement at the inauguration, which was attended by Gaddi Nashin Sant Niranjan Das of Dera Ballan, clearly indicated the dominance of the NRI groups, as the two front rows were largely occupied by 'tie-hat wearing people from abroad'.* Most of these NRIs were dressed formally, with all the men wearing a tie and hat, while the women, though dressed in the traditional salwar-kameez, were laden with gold ornaments, clearly marking them out from the local women.

The meeting began with Sant Surinder Das Baba thanking the Ravidassias settled all over the world for their generous donations and contribution for the *qaum* (community). Then he read out the amounts donated by various families and individuals settled abroad for the construction of the hospital, which had been built to commemorate the martyrdom of Sant Ramanand.

Many among the diaspora prominently displayed tricolour badges, symbolizing the Indian national flag, pinned to the lapel of their coats or kurtis, notably positioned above their glittering Ravidas badge. One of them expressed: 'We love our motherland, unlike *others*, and for us, the nation's integrity comes first.' This oft-repeated assertion on the notion of 'qaum' and '*watan*' (nation) by the diaspora needs a broader canvas of analysis.

It seemed that the community, especially the diaspora, wanted to fight the Jatt Sikhs head on. Their insistence on separation in religious matters, their donations to the deras to

---

* Ibid.

help them emerge as symbols of freedom from the shackles of the Jatt Sikhs, and their growing support for the Guru Ravidas Janam Asthan Mandir in Varanasi as the most important pilgrimage site for Ravidassias from all over the globe are some of the activities that highlight the overseas Ravidassias' growing influence and interest in their roots. Given that the diaspora space too has been marked by caste discriminations, there has been a palpable rivalry between the dominant Jatt Sikhs and subaltern community even overseas. The local/national caste imprints of discrimination in places of worship, for example, tend to play out there as well. The Vienna incident was perceived as the handiwork of the extremist elements. Hence, the assertion of some of the Ravidassia groups about the insignia and symbols of India. The overt flaunting of the Indianness could perhaps be seen as oblique reference to that and to project themselves as different. It is germane to underscore that these were early years of post Vienna incident and the collective wound of the community was still very raw and festering.

The Exit of Surinder Das

The death of Sant Ramanand in Vienna was a watershed moment not just for the Dera Ballan but also, in a way, for Dalit mobilization in the region. A memorial has been built at the site of his shooting in Vienna to honour his martyrdom. His departure left a significant void in the organization of the dera's activities, especially in building connections with overseas followers. Sant Niranjan Das, the gaddi nashin, is a simple, pious man of few words and lacked the necessary skills required to run an organization and meet its demands in an era of globalization and social media. Sant Ramanand had thus been a valuable asset for the dera, especially given his ability to manage its expansion and popularity among its NRI followers.

During the absence of the dera's main sants, such as when both the gaddi nashin and Sant Ramanand were on their trip to Vienna, the dera's affairs were managed by Surinder Das, affectionately known as Bawa Ji.

Surinder Das was born in a village called Suchi Pind in Jalandhar and graduated from Doaba College. His parents were devout followers and regular visitors to Dera Ballan. Surinder Das also regularly visited the dera with his parents. It is said that Sant Sarwan Das had blessed his mother, declaring that she would have two sons, and his mother had promised him that the elder one would be dedicated to the dera.

Following the death of Sant Ramanand, Surinder Das rose to prominence as he played an important role during the Vienna incident, when the dera received not just regional and national but also global media attention.

Surinder Das was seen as an active supporter of the campaign for total independence and a complete separation from the Sikh tradition, which was aggressively promoted in the wake of the shooting in Vienna. In 2010, when the dera announced the establishemnt of Ravidassia Dharma at Seer Goverdhanpur in Varanasi, and later in 2012 when Amritbani, a compilation of Guru Ravidas's bani, was declared as the holy book of the followers of the new religion, Surinder Das was perceived to be at the centre of the movement in close association with the diaspora segment of followers.

Surinder Das occupied the significant position left vacant by Ramanand until 2013-14. Most of the dera's publications, under the banner of Shri Guru Ravidas Janam Asthan Public Charitable Trust, including Amritbani Satguru Ravidas Maharaj Ji (Steek), were authored by 'Sant Surinder Das

Bawa Ji' and were translated into English by Shri Piare Lal. In these publications, Surinder Das was presented as the next in command after Sant Niranjan Das.

By 2014, however, Surinder Das was a name of the past in the dera, and a completely new set of people appeared to be in control of its everyday affairs. Surinder Das, after living in anonymity for a while, began his own independent dera called Ravidassia Dharam Prachar Asthan (RDPA) in Kahnpur, not far from Dera Ballan.

It appears that the campaign for a new religion and a new holy book, which sought to sever the age-old ties with Sikh rahit maryada—especially the central role of the Guru Granth Sahib—did not receive the same level of support and endorsement from the local Ravidassia community as it did from the affluent, particularly the NRI, followers of Dera Ballan. The centuries-old history of syncretism in the region proved to be both formidable and decisive. While it is true that the dera underwent significant changes after the Vienna incident, it quickly recognized the risks of pursuing a separatist path, especially in light of local sentiment.

It is believed that as part of the new strategy, Surinder Das was asked to go to Maharashtra to serve in another Guru Ravidas temple, which he refused to do and instead left Dera Ballan, only to reappear at Kahnpur with his new mission. While there is no doubt that Surinder Das commanded respect among the locals and had a significant following among the NRIs, the dera had reconsidered its future plans, factoring in local sentiments. In this new scheme and with a new team around Sant Niranjan Das, Surinder Das was left with no option but to exit.

There are several unsubstantiated stories about the exit of Surinder Das; one is that the gaddi nashin Niranjan Das was uncomfortable with the powerful role that Surinder Baba was playing along with the diaspora factions. It was felt that the leader was insecure about Surinder Das's rising stature in the aftermath of Sant Ramanand's demise. Following the Vienna incident, under pressure from local politicians, community leaders and business groups in Jalandhar, the dera initially went along with the separatist agenda, including the announcement of a new religion and a new holy book, and emphasizing an alternative rahit-maryada. However, by 2016-17, they realized that such a stand was just not tenable as it went against the cultural grain of the region and its sacred sensibilities.

Conversations with many elderly men and women who had been visiting Dera Ballan regularly for decades made it clear that they felt strongly against any attempt to sever ties with the Sikh rahit, particularly the reverence accorded to the Guru Granth Sahib. This was in spite of the fact that they resented the way the dominant upper castes subjugated them, and following the killing of Sant Ramanand, these wounds had been exacerbated. It is to be noted that in the wake of the Vienna shooting, the incidents of the replacement of the Bir with the Amritbani or a poster of Guru Ravidas were first reported from overseas and subsequently from many parts of Punjab, which heightened tensions and made the region's social harmony appear increasingly fragile.

Surinder Das's exit from Dera Ballan was the result of a combination of power politics within the dera and the interplay of local-global dynamics, which ultimately stalled the diaspora's demand for complete separation. This led to the birth of a new base for Surinder Das and the emergence of yet another dera in the region, not very far from Dera Ballan. This also explains the mushrooming of deras owing to multiple factors, and not just on account of religious differences. The political economy of the dera phenomenon thus becomes a critical lens to explore these developments.

Surinder Das's new dera has gradually evolved, and he now seems well settled. Banking on the support of his dedicated followers, both locally and abroad, he has established his new enterprise with great care and strategy. He continues to respect the Dera Ballan sants, especially Sant Sarwan Das, Sant Hari Das and Sant Ramanand, as is evident from the publicity materials of Ravidassia Dharam Prachar Asthan, which carry their photos and a photo of the Varanasi Janam Asthan temple at Seer Goverdhanpur.

Beginning with a modest dwelling with a few posters on the wall and a sangat asthal on the ground floor, Surinder Das's organizational acumen soon started yielding results. By 2018, he owned a high-end SUV, which was parked near the sangat asthal as proud display for the local devotees. It had been donated by one of his affluent followers from abroad. The RDPA now has an elaborate arrangement for langar as well as libraries well stocked with literature, not just on Guru Ravidas but also on Ambedkar, Phule and other Dalit icons. The main place of worship is on the first floor along with the library. Interestingly, the sanctum sanctorum too has posters and portraits of Ambedkar, placed almost at par with the religious items and symbols.

The RDPA has a dynamic social media wing, which documents all the activities, sangats and major visits and tours of Surinder Das. Recently, after the Covid pandemic, Surinder Das went on a whirlwind tour of Europe. Pictures and videos of his congregations, as well as of his airport welcomes by his followers, were widely circulated.

What distinguishes RDPA from other deras, even Dera Ballan, is that it presents itself as a modern, politically aware and progressive organization dedicated to the cause of Ravidassia history, culture and politics, not just in Punjab but also beyond. Its website and other social media platforms routinely discuss larger issues concerning the Dalits in general and Ravidassias in particular. When the renowned academic-activist and author Gail Omvedt passed away in 2021, the RDPA posted a condolence message on its website, reflecting its awareness and engagement with developments concerning the Dalit cause.

The RDPA library not only has books and materials on Dalits, it also has a special section dedicated to youth preparing for various competitive exams for government jobs, including the Punjab Civil Services, Central Civil Services, public sector banks, railways etc. The section is well-stocked with materials related to these exams, including newspapers and magazines. The Dera believes that merely being aware of one's identity and history is not enough; real empowerment will come when the youth of the community occupy important positions in the system.

The interesting part about Surinder Das's new enterprise is the name itself. The name 'Ravidassia Dharam Prachar Asthan' literally means the propagation of the tenets of Ravidassia Dharam, which became a bone of contention following the Vienna incident and ultimately forced Surinder Das to leave Dera Ballan. It is clear that he defiantly stood by his stance of actively supporting the movement for a separate religion and holy book exclusively containing the banis of Guru Ravidas in the aftermath of Ramanand's martyrdom.

His continued allegiance to Dera Ballan's sants like Sant Sarwan Das and Sant Hari Das shows that while he may have been dissatisfied and disagreed with the current leadership, he remained loyal to Dera Ballan itself. Every now and then, there are rumours about Surinder Das being seen in the dera or in the company of dera functionaries, and speculation about his possible return gains currency. Many local dera followers believe Surinder Das should return, as people recognize and acknowledge his dedication to the propagation of Ravidas Bani and his efficient handling of the English-speaking diaspora segment. His being young, educated and articulate has endeared him to the younger generation of the community, especially the NRIs.

Most of the publications of Dera Ballan till at least 2014 were under his editorship and supervision, and mention him as the author. He was instrumental in getting the Amritbani published in other languages such as Bangla, Telugu and Marathi, which was part of the dera's ambition of creating a national footprint.

When he left Dera Ballan, his close connections to the diaspora segment ensured that he continued to receive the patronage of the group. His new dera has flourished remarkably. His frequent trips abroad after Covid, as reported on the RDPA's website, tell the story of his success in creating and nurturing a social capital that seems to be paying dividends now.

While there has been much speculation about his return, so far there has been no concrete or authentic indication. As Dera Ballan is no longer actively pursuing the cause of a separate rahit-maryada or the propagation of Amritbani, while Surinder Das remains committed to it, the chances of his return look bleak, if not totally impossible.

From Ad-Dharmi to Ravidassia

When the great social reformer Babu Mangoo Ram Mugowalia was leading the movement for a new religion called Ad-Dharm in the early twentieth century, following his return from his foreign sojourn and his association with the Ghadarites in California, Dera Ballan, under the leadership of Baba Pipal Das, was operating from a few modest huts. Even then, Baba Pipal Das and his efforts towards the upliftment of his community were well known and acknowledged. As per one dera source, Babu Mangoo Ram came to meet Baba Pipal Das when the former was 'collecting the historical data of Maharishi Balmik Ji, Satguru Namdev Ji, Satguru Ravidas Ji, and Satguru Kabir Ji'.[7]

It is interesting to note the trajectories that these movements took over the course of nearly a century. While the movement for a separate religion, distinct from the mainstream religious traditions like Hinduism and Sikhism, proved successful initially with the recognition of Ad-Dharm as a separate religion and Ad-Dharmi as a separate religious group in the 1931 Census, Babu Mangoo Ram's initiative to unite the lower castes of the region under one umbrella did not last long. As Mangoo Ram was co-opted by the Congress party, the movement gradually lost momentum and petered out.

On his return from the US, Mangoo Ram saw the plight of the lower castes in the region and the discrimination they suffered at the hands of the dominant upper castes. He and his team initially tried taking the route of the Arya Samaj, given its claim of being caste-neutral. However, they soon realized the limitations of the existing frameworks. He then mobilized his people towards an independent alternative space called Ad-Dharm, meaning the religion of the original inhabitants, possibly drawing inspiration from similar movements elsewhere in the country, such as the Ad-Dravida movement in Tamil Nadu in the early twentieth century.

They established a new symbol, Soham, a new salutation, Jai Guru Dev, and authored a book called the Ad-Prakash Granth, consisting of 1,248 pages and featuring the hymns of Guru Ravidas, Maharishi Valmiki, Kabir and others. Mangoo Ram and his associates were working towards the consolidation of the untouchable castes of the region under the rubric of the new religion. However, it was clearly not yet an exclusive Ravidassia movement. It is true that the influential segment of the leadership belonged to the Chamar community, one of the largest and most influential among the Scheduled Castes, traditionally associated with 'polluting' leather work. Since Guru Ravidas also belonged to the Chamar community, it was natural that he gained prominence among the other saints revered by the Ad-Dharm community.

Post-independence, the Ad-Dharm movement was unable to sustain its momentum, and with the passing away of Mangoo Ram in 1980 it became rudderless. Other factors also contributed to its decline, the most significant being that Punjab's local politics and the dominance of the Congress party gradually co-opted many of the frontline leaders of the Ad-Dharm movement.

Secondly, under the government's reservation policy, the untouchables among the Hindus and Sikhs were eligible for various government schemes, including preference in jobs. This weakened the consolidation among the poor segments around the idea of Ad-Dharm as a separate religion.

Thirdly, the prominence given to Sant Ravidas alienated other groups among the Dalits who aligned with other religious gurus such as Valmiki. Fourthly, the diverse ideological and political leanings within the Ravidassia community, driven by the pressures of pragmatic politics, further deepened the fissures in the already divided group.

It is another matter that the label of Ad-Dharmi continued to have currency in the community, and a large number of castes associated with leather work still identify themselves as Ad-Dharmi. This demonstrates the deep, indelible and enduring impact of Mangoo Ram's work. Nonetheless, 'Ravidassia' gradually emerged as a new marker of identity among the Chamars of the region, especially among the followers of Dera Ballan.

This was most evident around the census year (2021), when various groups in Punjab, especially in the Doaba region, would articulate and advocate their allegiance to one or the other marker, Ad-Dharmi or Ravidassia. Many groups and deras that continued to identify with Ad-Dharm would exhort their fellow caste members to identify themselves as Ad-Dharmi and write to various government authorities petitioning for a separate identity.*

For instance, the Dera Khuralgarh, situated in the village of Kharali, Garhshanker, in the Hoshiarpur district of Punjab, was a significant Ravidassia dera but aligned more closely with the Ad-Dharm ideology and symbols. It encouraged its followers to identify as Ad-Dharmi rather than Ravidassia. Khuralgarh Dera is also known as Charan Choh Ganga Sri Guru Ravidas ji, as it was believed to have been visited by Guru Ravidas. A local legend recounts a miracle where a receding water body was restored after being touched by the guru's feet.

It is interesting that the Khuralgarh group continues to organize a temporary office and reception centre on

* The last census was done in 2011. It was expected in 2021 but was delayed due to the global pandemic. In anticipation of the 2021 census, there were these developments and movements around these markers.

every Ravidas Jayanti in Seer Goverdhanpur, prominently displaying posters of Mangoo Ram, Banta Ram Gheda and others, and highlighting the symbol Soham and other markers of Ad-Dharm.

Another group, by the name All India Ad-Dharma Mission, led by Shri Bharat Bhushan, son of Mewalal, Baba Banta Singh Gheda's associate from Uttar Pradesh, is based near the Janam Asthan temple, which is now recognized as the birthplace of Guru Ravidas, but has come under the control of Dera Ballan.

It appears that gradually these factions became highly competitive, with each of them attempting to corner a larger share of the Guru Ravidas legacy and the cultural capital associated with it. During the annual birth anniversary celebrations of Guru Ravidas held at the Janam Asthan temple, the three dominant factions occupy the landscape, and the varying degrees of their presence symbolize the struggle for power.

Dera Ballan has clearly outmanouevred the others, as they occupy centre stage, with the management of the celebration almost entirely under their control and ownership. Bharat Bhushan's group claims their centre marks the real birthplace of Guru Ravidas, but that claim has now been almost defeated, as the government has recognized the place under the control of Dera Ballan as the heritage site.

Located in close proximity to each other in Seer Goverdhanpur, these three groups reflect the rise and decline of three competing histories: Dera Ballan, with a monopoly over the Janam Asthan, emerges as the clear winner, followed by Bharat Bhusan's All India Ad Dharma Mission, while the Khuralgarh group lags far behind. The splendour of the Janam Asthan temple and the towering heights it has achieved over the years dwarf the modest centre of the Bharat Bhushan group and the makeshift office of the Khuralgarh group.

The sight of these three on the day of Ravidas Jayanti tells the story of two parallel narratives around the Ravidassia and Ad-Dharm communities, in which the one backed by Dera Ballan seems to have trumped everyone else.

Was Dera Sachkhand at Ballan always an exclusively Ravidassia dera? Yes and no. Yes, because it always, beginning with Baba Pipal Das, focused on Guru Ravidas's banis and shabads and gave primacy to him among the other bhakti saints. It is also true that this was despite the fact that they accorded the Guru Granth Sahib the highest place in their religious space.

Yet, as is always the case, especially in the region, traditions mutate and take alternative routes. The dera, however, never declared itself as a space *only* for the adherents of Ravidassia and continued to remain open to all. Many believe that Dera Sachkhand was initially an Udasi dera and the continued practices of performing aarti, ringing bells and blowing the conch give credence to this view.

What is clear is that the dera was always rooted in the tradition and history of Ravidas and made efforts to propagate his teachings and banis among its followers to inspire and motivate them and build their sense of self-worth. That the Guru Granth Sahib carries forty shabads of Guru Ravidas was seen as a recognition of the guru's spiritual status. Till this point, there was no problem. However, over the decades, things changed with the rise in the community's economic profile, the substantial growth of followers among the diaspora from the region and the resulting benefits from this.

More importantly, political marginalization despite substantial numerical strength, and the unrelenting caste discrimination they faced, pushed various groups to articulate a more clearly defined identity. Ravidassias were always the dominant segment of the Ad-Dharmi movement but the new environment eclipsed the nomenclature of Ad-Dharm. The rise of the Ravidassia identity grew from the community's demand for a fair share in the politics, culture and history of the region.

With the religious landscape becoming more and more competitive, the community launched a concerted effort to identify and recognize its saints, legends, icons and historical figures to resurrect its past. The faith and trust in a syncretic template that seemed to have betrayed their aspiration for equality because of their caste background eventually started to crack under its contradictions. The martyrdom of Sant Ramanand in Vienna in 2009 proved to be the tipping point for the unleashing of the frustration arising from their alienation and sense of denial.

Baba Pritam Das Dera with two nishaan sahibs

Even though Dera Ballan, or Dera Sachkhand, continues to command primacy and influence among Ravidassia followers, the Ravidassia identity is not a monolith. Although rooted in a similar caste background, the Ravidassia community displays a diversity of philosophies and perspectives.

Not very far from Dera Ballan, barely a kilometre and a half away, is the site of another Ravidassia dera—the Baba Pritam Das Dera—which acts as a modest yet powerful counterpoint. The proximity of these two deras encapsuates the religious history of the region—a history of argumentation, diversity and counterpoints, and of course, the resultant tug of war for power and authority.

The Pritam Das Dera catches one's attention from afar because of the unusual juxtaposition of two *nishaan sahibs*, religious insignia, mounted atop two towering poles that seem to touch the sky. One nishaan is of Hari, representing the Ravidassia identity, and the other is of Ek Onkar, the symbol of the Sikh tradition. Given the controversy surrounding the idea of a new religion called Ravidassia Dharma, propagated by Dera Ballan in the aftermath of the Vienna incident, the sight of the two nishaan sahibs together at Baba Pritam Das Dera instantly stands out.

Sant Baba Nirmal Das ji, or Baba Jaure as he is affectionately and popularly called by his followers, is the current gaddi nashin of this dera. Baba Nirmal Das believes in coexistence rather than separation. Following the Vienna incident, during the cremation of Sant Ramanand, Dera Ballan, in an act of defiance, did not follow the code of conduct as prescribed under the Sikh rahit maryada. Baba Nirmal Das, on the other hand, was opposed to any disrespect or deviation from the rahit maryada of the Guru Granth Sahib.

He believes in the coexistence of all religions and in articulating the identity of Ravidas while maintaining that there should be no weakening of the age-old ties with Sikhism and particularly the Guru Granth Sahib. It is precisely to drive home this message that his dera has two nishaan sahibs in its premises—to underscore the unity among the communities of the region. He believes that propagating the idea of only one community, guru or sant would fragment or weaken the larger community of Dalits.

The Baba Pritam Das Dera clearly follows and gives primacy to the Sikh maryada and the Guru Granth Sahib. There is ample evidence of this in Baba Jaure's private office, where the sacred symbol Ek Onkar is prominently dispayed on the walls alongside posters of Ambedkar, Baba Pritam Das and Guru Ravidas.

The dera of Jaure Baba differs on most counts from Dera Ballan. For example, while Dera Ballan advocates the supremacy and separate identity of Ravidassia, the Pritam Das Dera follows the path of coexistence and accords primacy to the Sikh maryada and the Guru Granth Sahib.

Dera Ballan compiled the shabads and verses of Guru Ravidas into a new holy book, known as Amritbani, but the dera of Baba Jaure does not subscribe to this, as he believes in borrowing from all sources—mainly from Sikhism but also from Hinduism. Dera Ballan has invested heavily and almost exclusively in Seer Goverdhanpur in Varanasi, as Guru Ravidas was born there. In contrast, Dera Baba Pritam Das, under the leadership of Baba Jaure, has invested in the city of Haridwar in Uttarakhand, where Baba Jaure undertakes an annual pilgrimage along with his followers.

Baba Jaure is the president of the Shri Guru Ravidas Sadhu Sampradaye Society, which claims to have some 300 deras from the region as its members. Its centre in Haridwar is called Bhagwan Ravidas Ashram, Begumpura Nirmala Chhauni, and was built in 1960. More recently, in 2011, the society constructed a huge gate called Shri Guru Ravidas Ji Memorial Gate at Jatwara, near the village of Jawalapur, which leads to Har ki Pauri in Haridwar.

While Dera Ballan organizes the Begumpura Express to Varanasi on the occasion of Ravidas Jayanti, Dera Pritam Das organizes a pilgrimage to Haridwar with its followers around the same time, in conjunction with the Damri yaatra at Har ki Pauri. The dera also organizes the Ravidas Shahi Asnaan on the occasion of the Kumbh Mela, which is well attended by followers from Punjab, other states and from abroad.

Baba Jaure laments the fact that Dera Ballan unilaterally decided to create a new holy book and found a new religion without consulting other communities. On the issue of the nomenclature—Ad-Dharmi versus Ravidassia—he clearly favours the former. Curiously, one rarely sees the word 'Ad-Dharmi' in the literature and publicity materials of his dera. Could this be because the word 'Ravidassia' has gained currency among the youth and especially the diaspora? Given that, by his own admission, more than seven lakh of his followers are settled abroad and contribute significantly to his deras and other organizations, he probably sensed the pulse of the growing mobilization and worked accordingly.

He has bought land in Khuralgarh, where he plans to set up a branch as he sees no competition with the existing Khuralgarh Dera. Baba Jaure is clearly politically savvy and strategically positions himself and his dera as being rooted in Ravidassia identity, but at the same time, he maintains good relationships with other faiths and traditions. In Punjab they continue to demonsrate their allegiance to Sikh tradition, while in Haridwar they emphasize their linkages with Hinduism. Like Dera Ballan, they refer to Guru Ravidas's birthplace in Varanasi as a mandir, not a dera. This adaptability reflects the deras' keen temporal astuteness.

In Jalandhar city, on the birth anniversary of Sant Valmiki in 2022, every nook and corner was covered with posters commemorating Maharishi Valmiki. What was particularly striking was Baba Jaure's presence on almost all the posters alongside Ambedkar and other Bhakti saints and gurus, including Guru Ravidas and Guru Nanak. In contrast, Dera Ballan's posters typically featured Guru Ravidas, Ambedkar, Mirabai and sometimes Sant Valmiki, but seldom included Guru Nanak or any Hindu gods or goddesses.

Baba Jaure's presence reflects the outreach and connections he has established through his organization with other caste groups from within the Dalit communities, who have felt alienated and hold grievances against Dera Ballan's emphasis on the exclusivity of the Ravidassia identity. Baba Jaure has sought to connect with this discontented group in the years following the Vienna incident and the martyrdom of Ramanand. In fact, his dera sent a specially decorated bus to join the *shobha yaatra** in the main city, organized by various Valmiki groups.

As a visible counterpoint to Dera Ballan and despite some controversial moments, Baba Jaure's dera adds to the mysterious world of new possibilities and politics around the institution of the dera in Punjab.

Dera Ballan today and the neighbouring ecosystem

Dera Ballan today appears quieter and more settled. The restlessness and the air of protest that was so palpable in the aftermath of the Vienna incident has gradually cooled down. At least so it appears. During the pandemic, the dera had to cancel its annual train journey to Varanasi on the birth anniversary of Guru Ravidas. However, the journey resumed in 2022 and made headlines, as the Election Commission of India (ECI) had to postpone the date of the state assembly election in Punjab to accommodate the pilgrimage.[8] This added to the status of Dera Ballan and demonstrated the clout that it wielded, as it was on their request that the ECI changed the election dates.

---

* A large procession organized to commemorate the sants with great fanfare.

The dera was already in the news due to the steady stream of political heavyweights making a beeline there to seek their support in the run-up to the crucial state assembly election. During his visit in December 2021, the then chief minister Charanjit Singh Channi announced several ambitious projects, including the establishment of a research centre at Ballan dedicated to the study of Guru Ravidas's teachings and the Amritbani. Of the project cost of Rs 50 crore, a cheque for Rs 25 crore was handed over to the dera. He also announced the formation of a Ravidas Bani Adhiyan Kendra Prabandhak Committee headed by Gaddi Nashin Sant Niranjan Das of Dera Ballan.

On another occasion, on the night before the Republic Day celebration and flag unfurling at Jalandhar, Chief Minister Channi decided to spend the night at Dera Sachkhand at Ballan, sleeping on the floor of dera head Sant Niranjan Das's room. Later, at Phagwara, while addressing a meeting of Congress party workers, he said, 'I received calls from a couple of officers who advised me against staying at the dera, but I said if I will be booked for staying there then let it be so, but I shall stay there only. I slept on the floor in Baba ji's room and listened to his sermons, which were soothing'.[9]

It is another matter that none of these gestures paid any dividends, as not only did his party lose, but Mr Channi himself lost both the seats he contested from by a huge margin in the 2022 assembly elections. The political regime change in the state led to the stalling of the projects that had been announced by the then chief minister.

While Dera Ballan has become quieter in recent years, the two other distinct centres for the articulation of the Ravidassia identity in the vicinity remain steadfast in their original ideological positions. The dera of Surinder Das has expanded, and its popularity among overseas followers has risen, if his travel itinerary to overseas destinations post Covid is any indication. Indeed, he has been on the move since the Covid travel restrictions were lifted.

It is important to recall here that Surinder Das's role following the Vienna attack, coupled with his overenthusiasm for the movement for separate religion—largely backed by the diaspora segment—created a rift between him and the dera's management, ultimately leading to his exit. That he not only survived but also created a niche for himself and his little organization is a reflection of the fact that many believed in him and wished to stand by him.

Interestingly, he continues to revere Sant Sarwan Das. Photos, calendars and events to celebrate the birth and death anniversaries of Sant Ramanand and other sants, but not the current gaddi nashin Sant Niranjan Das, at Surinder Baba's dera are a reminder of his fractured affiliation with Dera Ballan. In other words, while the sants of Dera Ballan remain a common glue, differences survive and even prosper.

The same is the case with Baba Jaure's dera. Its disagreement with Dera Ballan continues. The dera, known for prominently displaying two nishaan sahibs on its premises, has differed from Dera Ballan and its sants on two counts: first, for deviating from Sikh tenets, and second, for abandoning the Ad-Dharmi movement and instead championing the Ravidassia identity.

It is for these reasons that the dera appears to align with others that support the Ad-Dharmi movement, including Satinder Heera of Charan Choḥ Ganga, Khuralgarh. Baba Jaure and others advocate maintaining the community's age-old ties with Sikhism while also nurturing its cause in collaboration with Hindu organizations. It's no surprise then that while

Dera Ballan went to Varanasi looking for its roots, the Pritam Das Dera went to Haridwar on a pilgrimage.

Its vocabulary and publications clearly reflect a desire to forge amicable relations with both major religious streams, Hinduism and Sikhism. It is precisely for this reason that the sant of this dera is often targeted by hardliners, who accuse him of working for the 'others' rather than for the community.

Dera Sachkhand at Ballan, however, continues to remain a major force pursuing the cause of the Ravidassia identity. The dera remains steadfast in its ideological position that the Ravidassia community must be recognized as a distinct identity, and every effort should be made to establish and strengthen this identity under the revered name of Guru Ravidas.

Of course, there are counter-narratives to this monolithic version, as we have seen. Yet, it seems that Dera Ballan, under the Ravidassia banner, will continue to serve as a colossal tower of light for not just the local community, but also for the pan-Indian and global communities, especially those who, in the past or present, have been linked to leather work within India's caste system.

5

The Making of a Pilgrimage: Dera Ballan in Varanasi

Pilgrimages hold a religious connotation. In popular imagination, they are about a divine place, a sacred site, which people wish to someday visit. However, these sites are part of a broader network of identity politics that often remains muted and unnoticed by ordinary actors—those who participate in the events without being fully aware of the underlying politics and power dynamics at play.

These places carry with them a bewildering mix of myths, histories, folklore and local stories. They often bridge the gap between the local and larger narratives, constantly working to weave together the innumerable loose threads of the multiple narratives that are continually added to their own repertoire of myth and legend.

They are, at one level, of critical significance to their believers, for they provide them with a sense of connection with a cosmic umbrella that extends to their ancestors. So, Kashi and Haridwar, the Golden Temple and Nankana Sahib, Mecca and Madina—indeed, any sacred site is much more than its visible temporality. These sites stand as signposts of memory, of pride, of solidarity and sustenance, of history and counter-history for those who repose faith in them.

In other words, in the political-economic matrix of a pilgrimage site, religion may be a central theme, perhaps a major running thread, but it is not everything.

Jalandhar and Varanasi are separated by a distance of about 1200 kilometres. Culturally too, they are miles apart in terms of their world views. It would not be wrong to say that Punjab appears broadly as the antonym to the religio-cultural *weltanschauung* of Varanasi.

If Varanasi is one of the major cultural centres of Hinduism and its rich traditions, the land of Punjab has, over the centuries, emerged as the site of alternative discourse and philosophy and the birth of a new faith called Sikhism, which questioned some of the premises and precepts of Hinduism. Interestingly, Punjab has retained its culture of questioning and rebellion. As a result, multiple traditions flourish and prosper, creating a rich and more syncretic socio-religious landscape on the ground—one that is perhaps more diverse than anywhere else.

Of course, the region has had its share of conflicts and contestations, but that is only natural. Broadly, it has a deep and solid history of accommodation and coexistence, which defines its cultural genotype. The legacy of togetherness and interconnection is so robust that it eventually trumps all attempts at divisiveness. The ethos of syncretism, the land's prototype civilizational commitment, always triumphs in the end.

As Dera Sachkhand Ballan in Jalandhar gradually gained strength and momentum over the years, its ties to Sant Ravidas and his association with the city of Varanasi gained even greater significance. Varanasi is believed to be the birthplace of Sant

Ravidas. It was only natural that the city, which is considered one of the most sacred places for Hindus, became the site of an alternative imagination as well. Yet, it was not easy—the process of gaining recognition and acceptance has been both tedious and lengthy.

It took decades to reach where it is today. The establishment of the Shri Guru Ravidas Janam Asthan Mandir (SGRJSM) at Seer Goverdhanpur in Varanasi is, in a sense, a remaking of history through imagining a pilgrimage for a community that was always peripheral in India's caste framework.

Shri Guru Ravidas Janam Asthan Mandir: a brief history

As the stature of Dera Sachkhand Ballan and its gurus grew, beginning in the 1920s, efforts to construct visible signposts signalling a coming of age of the community gained wider appeal among the followers of the dera, who were spread not just in Punjab but all over the world. It is believed that the then dera chief, Sant Sarwan Das, had a dream about an *imli* (tamarind) tree near the Banaras Hindu University (BHU) campus. It is notable that most of the hagiographical accounts of the life of Ravidas refer to his association with this tree species. In this dream, Sarwan Das received a divine message revealing that the imli tree was the very one under which Guru Ravidas had practiced *saadhna*, or meditation, and delivered his sermon on Begumpura.

As one of the booklets of the dera mentions, 'The sacred task of perpetuating the memory of Guru Ji at Banaras and giving a befitting memorial in his name was undertaken by the spiritual, visionary and revolutionary saint sri 108 Sant Sarwan Das ji of Dera Sachkhand Ballan. He made strenuous efforts

The main worship place of Dera Sachkhand Ballan

The samadhis or the memorial sites of the Sants of the Dera Ballan
in the Dera premises

The gold-plated palanquin donated by a diaspora group to the Dera Ballan

A calendar and video shop near the Dera Ballan

One of the covers of a video promoting the Ravidassia identity

Adjacent to Dera Ballan, this is the Baba Pritam Das Dera that emphasizes the unity between the Sikh and Ravidassia identities, as demonstrated here in the two insignia on their premises

The author with L.R. Balley, a prominent Ambedkarite from Punjab, and Manohar Mahey, a former trustee of Dera Ballan and a distinguished citizen of Boota Mandi—at the former's residence in Jalandhar in 2017

The locomotive engine of the Indian Railways being decorated as the Begumpura Express by Ravidassias—Jalandhar Railway station, 2014

The main Guru Ravidas temple at Seer Goverdhanpur at Varanasi

The imli tree (tamarind or *tamarindus Indica*) near the Ravidas temple in Seer Goverdhanpur, Varanasi, believed to be the place where Guru Ravidas worked on leather to convey the message of *Man changa toh kathauti me ganga* (if the mind is pure, the sacred Ganga can be found in the water of the platter that one uses to clean leather)

A bookshop largely selling Dalit literature close to the Ravidas Jayanti fair in Varanasi near the temple

A bhajan mandali or a group of folk singers, from Sagar, Madhya Pradesh, singing songs in praise of Guru Ravidas

A calendar–poster shop at Seer Goverdhanpur in Varanasi depicting a largely saguni (Krishna devotee) avatar of Ravidas, quite in contrast to Punjab's *nirguni* portrayal

Mahant Bharat Bhushan at his abode near Seer Goverdhanpur, Varanasi, which he claims is the original birthplace of Guru Ravidas

Ambedkar is like a pan-Indian identity umbrella. Here, a Ravidas follower rests near a shop at the mela ground in Seer Goverdhanpur on the occasion of Ravidas Jayanti

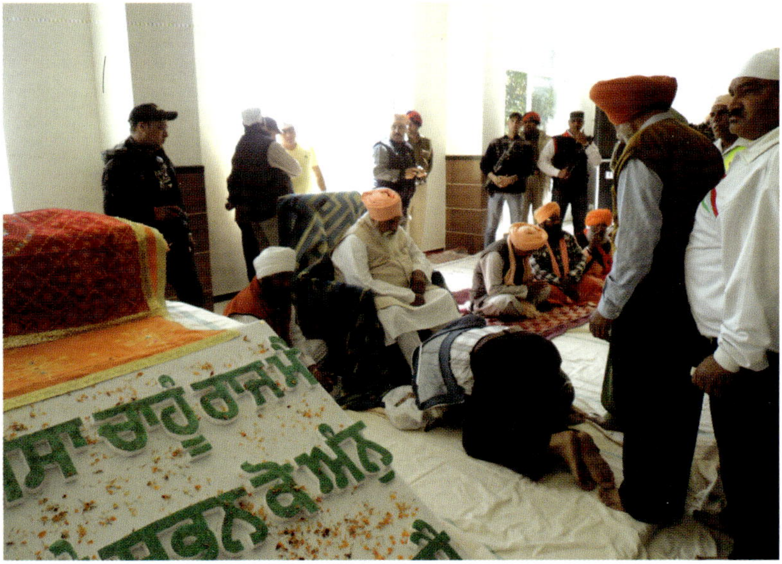

Followers queue up to seek blessings from Sant Niranjan Das, the present chief of the Dera Ballan. This is in Kapur–Dhepur near Ballan in 2013 on the occasion of the inauguration of a hospital in the name of the slain Sant Ramanand

to make Bani of Guru Ravidas ji popular among the socially backward and downtrodden people. He thought his job to be incomplete until the place where Guru Ravidas ji gave the sermon of Begumpura was traced out and a suitable monument built there.'

The concept of 'Begumpura' was propounded by Guru Ravidas in his banis to describe a utopia—a place where there would be peace and no conflict, an ideal space free from discrimination and suffering.

Following this sacred dream, Sant Sarwan Das initiated concerted efforts on the ground, entrusting Sant Hari Das, his second-in-command, and a few others from the dera to travel to Varanasi. Their mission was to locate the site of the imli tree and then lay the foundation stone of the temple. The team went to Varanasi and visited the BHU campus, on the outskirts of the city. An imli tree and other landmarks in the locality of Seer Goverdhanpur were identified by the team of surveyors from Dera Ballan as the closest match to the depiction provided by Sant Sarwan Das.

The land around the imli tree was purchased, and the foundation stone for the temple was laid on 14 June 1965 by Sant Hari Das along with a group of dera sevadaars and other functionaries. The project got off to a slow start given the difficulties in clearing the area and ensuring access for building materials through the congested lanes surrounding the site chosen for building the temple. Major support came from Ravidassias settled overseas, who were keen to have a befitting place of pilgrimage built at the birthplace of their revered guru.

Surmounting all difficulties and thanks to the dedicated efforts of Dera Ballan, the first phase of the Janam Asthan Mandir was completed in 1972. This phase was led by Sant Garib Das of Dera Ballan. On 22 February 1974, the temple was inaugurated with the installation of a statue of Guru Ravidas. To commemorate this milestone event, a large contingent of sants from various deras of Punjab along with prominent community leaders from the region accompanied Sant Garib Das to Varanasi. The occasion was also marked by the installation of a statue of Sant Sarwan Das in the temple precincts.

Shri Guru Ravidas Janam Asthan Public Charitable Trust (Regd), headquartered at Dera Ballan, worked to complete the remaining construction work. The second phase was completed in 1993 and culminated in the installation of a golden *kalash* on the top of the temple on 7 April 1994, in the presence of Kanshi Ram, the founder of the Bahujan Samaj Party (BSP), and various dera sants and devotees.

The site rose to prominence when the Shri Sant Sarwan Dass Charitable Trust, based in the UK, expressed the desire to build a monumental gate dedicated to Guru Ravidas in the city, leading to the newly constructed mandir at Seer Goverdhanpur. This project was undertaken by the trust, and soon a huge gate at Lanka crossing was built and inaugurated in July 1998 by K. R. Naraynan, the then President of India.

As the mandir gained prominence, the number of visitors increased significantly—not only from Punjab and north-western states likes Haryana and Himachal, but also from areas surrounding Varanasi and other states across the country. On the occasion of Ravidas Jayanti, a large number of devotees and followers of the guru come to the city from all over the world, adding to the growing stature of the site, which until the 1970s and 1980s was barely known.

Over the years, the trust has continued to expand its base in the area with the addition of a four-storey ashram (for pilgrims to stay in) and a huge langar hall to serve free food to visitors.

The growing popularity of the pilgrimage site is evident from the fact that the number of bogies on the special Begumpura Express, arranged by the dera to take devotees from Jalandhar City to Varanasi each year for Ravidas Jayanti, has progressively increased. A journey that began as a small dream, with a few dera followers booking a compartment in the regular Jammu Tawi to Varanasi train that passed through Jalandhar, has now grown into a big event, with the booking of an entire special train, named the 'Begumpura Express', from the Indian Railways. The story of this journey is remarkable, reflecting the rise of an ethos of 'communitas' among the Ravidassias. The train is a sort of history on wheels that mirrors the rising stature of the SGRJSM as a pilgrimage centre.

The role of the overseas population of Ravidassias from Punjab in this success story has been enormous. In 2007, followers based in several European countries donated a golden palanquin as a token of their respect and as a sacred contribution to the pilgrimage site. The palanquin was taken out in a religious procession, which began from Dera Ballan in Jalandhar, continued thorugh various towns in Punjab, Haryana, Delhi and Uttar Pradesh, and culminated at the Janam Asthan Mandir in Varanasi. When the golden palanquin reached Varanasi, Mayawati, the then chief minister of Uttar Pradesh, presided over the event to mark its installation on Guru Ravidas Jayanti (21 February 2008).

The enthusiasm for the mandir in Varanasi has been so great that there has been an overwhelming response to contribute towards its magnificence and grandeur. Sant Ramanand had always dreamt of the temple having gold-plated walls. His wish was partially fulfilled when, under the first phase of the project, the dome was gold-plated. Sant Ramanand was so deeply committed to this project that he even composed a poem exhorting the people to donate and contribute generously:

Chalo Banaras sadhu sangat ji
Ik itihaas rachauna hai,
Guru Ravidass de Mandir nuu,
Sone di vich marahauna hai.
Katra katra mil ke jiddan,
Ik samundar ban jaanda
Patti patti jor ke ik,
Sone da Mandir ban jaanda

Let us go to Banaras
All saints and devotees,
To create history
We shall make a temple of gold
For our revered Guru Ravidas.
Like drop by drop one creates an ocean
We shall donate bit by bit
To create a temple of gold
In honour of our Guru Ravidass[1]

Vienna incident and SGRJSM, Varanasi as centre stage

Over time, the Janam Asthan Mandir in Varanasi has emerged as the centre of Dera Sachkhand Ballan's activities. In a sense, this has been both a conscious and strategic move by the dera. For decades, it operated in a localized manner, but as a growing sense of communitas emerged, breaking regional, national and global boundaries, it was only natural for the dera to need a larger platform. This expansion of the dera beyond Ballan in Jalandhar has been facilitated by the influential diaspora segment of its devotees settled all over the world.

In 2009, when the Vienna tragedy struck and the dera lost one of its prominent sants, Sant Ramanand, much of the followers' initial anguish was localized. However, as emotions gradually settled, in the following year, 2010, SGRJSM witnessed one of the dera's most daring acts in terms of its expression of autonomy and a separation from its roots.

The declaration of a new, separate religion and the release of the holy book Amritbani were organized on the occasion of Ravidas Jayanti at Seer Govardhanpur. While the decisions were taken at the dera's Jalandhar headquarters, they were made public in Varanasi. This speaks volumes about the growing significance of Varanasi not just as a major pilgrimage centre but also as a symbol of the dera's long-cherished desire to be recognized as a significant religious formation. And there could be no more fitting a place than Varanasi, one of the foremost pilgrimage centres of the Hindus, to announce to the world the arrival of the community called Ravidassia.

Varanasi, in that sense, became the global stage for the Ravidassia movement led by Dera Ballan. On the occasion of Ravidas Jayanti, the number of devotees coming from overseas destinations multiplied. So much so that the hotel industry in Varanasi eagerly anticipated the event, as it brought good business. Individuals, families and groups of Ravidassias from abroad would book hotels well in advance to attend the function.

The dera organization and leadership are well aware of the pivotal role played by the diaspora segment, both economically and socio-politically, in their rise to prominence. Indeed, the significance of this segment was clearly visible as the Begumpura Express began to offer luxury coaches for them, catering to their lifestyle and convenience. The train is otherwise an equal space but for these special coaches. Despite its obvious irony, the special arrangement by the dera for its wealthy overseas devotees stands out as a reminder that the dera is not entirely immune to this-worldly practical considerations in its ambitious journey towards a more organized and independent existence.

Coach no. S-8: Begumpura Express as spectacle

7 February 2017 was a special day. The Begumpura Express was to begin its journey on this day from Jalandhar to Varanasi. I had witnessed the pomp and festivity that marked the eve of Ravidas Jayanti several times, but this was the first time I was travelling on the train to be part of the pilgrimage.

The special pass issued by the dera indicated that I had been allocated a berth in Coach S-8. I arrived at the railway station, as instructed by the dera functionaries, to a familiar yet captivating sight—thunderous drumbeats, loudspeakers playing songs glorifying the sants of Dera Ballan and Ravidassias from all over the world—men, women and children—thronging the station, singing and dancing as if possessed and in a trance amidst the collective chants of *Jo bole so Nirbhai, Guru Ravidas Maharaj ki jai*, a popular salutation of the Ravidassia, repeated a regular intervals.

The Begampura Express was often at the platform much earlier than its scheduled departure, and for most of the day, the Jalandhar station would be teeming with Ravidassias, with thousands gathering outside just to see the train off. This time wasn't any different. As the passengers boarded their respective coaches, those outside shouted slogans, sang bhajans with folded hands, and touched the chugging train as if the coaches were an extension of the divine.

The NRI devotees were visible from a distance, conspicuous by their outfits—hats, ties and formal attire—and touristy gadgets including sophisticated cameras. Many of them were travelling with their families, including teens and even little kids. While the older generation of women wore the traditional Punjabi salwar-kameez, the younger generation were in jeans and casual attire, wearing looks of bemusement, excitement and amusement all rolled into one. The older men and women mixed with the locals in singing, dancing and slogan shouting, while Generation Next looked at them in awe, clicking pictures and every now and then mimicking their gestures.

The atmosphere was charged with camaraderie and bonhomie. The bogies were decorated with festoons and colourful balloons. Posters of Dera Ballan sants, Mirabai and other Bhakti saints and contemporaries of Ravidas were pasted all over the train. A huge poster of Guru Ravidas adorned the front of the train engine, and the main sant of Dera Ballan inaugurated the event, announcing the beginning of the journey. Drumbeats reached a crescendo, and with the thunderous salutation of '*Jo bole so Nirbhai Satguru Ravidass Maharaj ki jai*', the train slowly departed.

As we settled into our respective berths, I found my immediate co-passengers to be two very interesting people—Gita Rani, forty-three, from Hoshiarpur, and Mohan Lal, fifty-eight, from Nawanshahr. Gita Rani was a regular visitor to Dera Ballan. Her husband was a popular Sufi singer on YouTube, and she proudly informed me that he was the chairperson of the Begumpura Tiger Force of Hoshiarpur.*

* A band of followers basically connoting allegiance to the teachings of Guru Ravidas and the word Begumpur has been borrowed from Guru Ravidass's shabad.

She was well versed in Urdu, which she had learnt from her grandfather, and she worshipped at a local pir-mazaar. The hybridity of faiths she embodied had a very interesting and vibrant family history. Her mother-in-law and father-in-law were followers of Baba Balaknath, while she, being a Ravidassia, was inspired by the stories of Sufi sants such as Baba Farid and others shared by her grandfather. Her interest in Sufism and Islam was so strong that she wished to visit Mecca and Medina at least once in her lifetime.

'Ravidassia is my qaum,' she said, and within that there were various shades that illuminated her spiritual journey. At the mazaar where she worships, her *murshid* or guru was a Brahmin by caste but later converted to Islam. She was going to Varanasi to seek *dua* or *rahmat* (blessings).

Listening to Gita's story felt like experiencing the history of South Asia, with its fluidity of faiths, through an evocative personal narrative. Her clear understanding of various faiths and her effortless disregard for boundaries had an innocence shaped by an upbringing in a culture that emphasized coexistence and mutuality over segregation.

Mohan Lal, in contrast, was a rather quiet person. He kept to himself for most of the journey. But on my insistence, he finally opened up. He belonged to the district of Nawanshahr. In 2014, he took naamdaan from the baba ji of Ballan, and since then, he has been a regular devotee of Dera Ballan and participates in its activities. His son lives in the UK.

In his hometown, he visits a Sikh dera called Dera Baba Jaora Singh, but he told me that his neigbourhood has about 500 Ravidassia families, and all of them keep the Amritbani in their homes. Although the dera he visits has only the Guru Granth Sahib, other Ravidassia gurudwaras have both the Guru Granth Sahib and the Amritbani.

He had visited Varanasi a couple of years ago and had wished for a grandchild. As custom demanded, he had tied a sacred thread around the imli tree as a symbol of his wish. On this visit he was going to untie the thread, or *dhaga kholne*, as his wish had been fulfilled. He had also donated a gold ring to Dera Ballan.

As the train sped up, the passengers gradually settled down. Amidst the distribution of water bottles, snacks and tea by the sevadaars of each coach, some women began singing bhajans in praise of Guru Ravidas, while the younger lot busied themselves with their mobiles.

At every designated halt of the train, groups of people from the community would be gathered at the platform, often accompanied by bands in dazzling outfits, to welcome and greet the passengers and to honour the Dera sants and other functionaries of the dera. When the chief, Sant Niranjan Das, and his team disembarked at the station, men, women and children garlanded them, sought their blessings by touching their feet and took selfies. Still others would grasp the train's windows and touch them with their foreheads as a sign of respect and to seek blessings. The train in these moments was transformed into a sacred entity, far beyond its temporal significance.

Back in the coach, every now and then there would be a loud salutation or *jaikaara* of *Jo bole so Nirbhai* by the younger lot, with others joining in, and this would echo throughout the train. The few coaches carrying the NRIs lose out on these moments of bonhomie, camaraderie and the sheer thrill of being part of a unique journey. The NRI coaches, I was informed, were added much later, when the number of overseas passengers increased, and many began visiting with their families, including young children and elderly members who required the comfort they were used to. Recognizing their influence and growing financial support, the management decided to add a few special coaches.

Thanks to a sympathetic dera functionary who recognized me, I was able to sit in an NRI coach for a few hours. I met some of these influential people, including doctors, businessmen and media barons, all from the Ravidassia community, who had come from all over the globe, but largely from Europe, especially the UK. The narratives behind their journey to Ballan and Varanasi were driven by similar emotions—a deep sense of nostalgia for their roots. However, this nostalgia was different; it carried an unmistakable vibe of an urge to 'get even', be it symbolically.

Older folks would recount tales of the discrimination they had suffered before they migrated to alien lands looking for opportunities; many others remembered their parents' experiences of exploitative caste practices in Punjab. The younger lot, in contrast, appeared to be much less emotional but were well-versed in the history of their community and their Ravidassia identity. Ms Badhan and Ms Aheer, two young professionals—one a doctor and the other a lawyer—came across as articulate and familiar with the history of Dera Ballan and the Ravidassia movement in general. In fact, they took issue with the use of the word 'Dalit', as they found it to be pejorative and demeaning. Instead, they preferred 'Ravidassia' as their identity.

As the two young women conversed with great poise and eloquence, their parents watched silently but with visible pride, confidence and reassurance writ large across their faces. Meanwhile, the train had stopped at yet another designated halt, and it was time for me to return to my coach as the sun was setting. A mendicant folk singer—a familiar and popular figure among the pilgrims of the Begumpura Express for many years—was playing the *khanjadi*, a type of musical instrument, and singing the song *Videsh me charcha Ballan di*, meaning Ballan is famous even in foreign lands. There could not have been a more fitting setting for the song.

As I returned to my coach, I wondered whether the young Ravidassias settled abroad understood the deeper context of the word 'Dalit' back in their ancestors home, where it stands as a potent and established term in place of words like 'Harijan'.

This has been a remarkable journey, an incredible achievement, given that it all began just about three decades ago (around 1984), when a few individuals associated with the dera booked a few berths in the Howrah Mail and set out on a journey to Varanasi to celebrate Ravidas Jayanti. A few years later, they booked a full coach, then a few bogies, and finally, by 1994, a special train called the Begumpura Express—formerly known as the 12238 Jammu Tawi-Varanasi Express—was started to take Ravidassia pilgrims to Varanasi.

The train, in the process, became iconic and a part of history. It became a bridge between Punjab and Uttar Pradesh, thereby linking the two almost contrary cultural and geographic landscapes and people. It would therefore be naïve to mistake the sights and experiences surrounding the Ravidas Jayanti yaatra as run of the mill. Behind the seeming ordinariness lies an enormous web of networks, identity politics and the incredible journey of a community that has waited on the margins for centuries. Riding on a history of hard-earned industriousness and prosperity, the Ravidassia arrives in Varanasi not merely as a pilgrim, but to stake a claim in the public sphere, that too as exalted a place as Varanasi.

The imli tree and the floating stone

In the majestic Janam Asthan Mandir area in Seer Goverdhanpur, there are two important sacred spots—one is the imli tree, adjacent to the temple, which was found by the dera team, and the other is the legendary stone that was, it is believed, made to float in the river Ganga by Guru Ravidas when he was challenged by the Brahmins of Kashi to display his divine powers. The area around the sacred imli tree is now well lit and decorated. Men, women and children tie sacred threads around the tree, light earthen lamps and offer flowers to express their reverence for their supreme Guru.

On an ordinary day, the Janam Asthan Mandir is visited by people, almost always Dalit, not just from as far as Haryana, Himachal and Punjab, but also from nearby towns and villages of Uttar Pradesh and Bihar. During one of my visits there, I met a group of young men, all from the Ravidassia community, who had travelled from Haryana to pay their obeisance to their guru. The young men told me they were from the Begumpura Tiger Force unit in Kurukshetra (in Haryana). They had donated Rs 1000 towards what was mentioned on the receipt as langar seva.

The local visitors from the region were a mixed lot, many of them from the Valmiki *sampradaya*, or faith-community, and some even identified themselves as Kabir panthis. The temple trust offers all visitors langar and accomodation in a nearby dharamshala. On an average, the trust receives dozens of such visitors a day, with the numbers picking up considerably during Ravidas Jayanti. The individual donations varied from a hundred rupees to several thousands. One of the visitors expressed his sentiments in these words: 'These sites are our identity markers, reminders of our glorious history, people and our saints. If we do not support it who will? We want these to grow and be visible.'

In the innermost part of the temple lies the sacred stone, encased in a transparent box, which the devotees touch to seek blessings. It is believed to be the very stone that Guru Ravidas made float in the river Ganga. According to popular legend, the Brahmins of the city were unhappy with the rising popularity of the sant from a lower caste and complained to the king. In response, the king invited Guru Ravidas to his court and asked both him and the Brahmins to demonstrate their sacred powers by making a stone float in the Ganga. It is said that, despite their efforts, the Brahmins failed, while Guru Ravidas succeeded in making the stone float. The king became a disciple of Guru Ravidas and instructed the Brahmins to respect his teachings.

This legend is recounted in various booklets and publicity materials of the dera and other organizations devoted to the legacy of Guru Ravidas. Such legends serve as powerful unifiers, binding people from varied regions, linguistic backgrounds and states under the umbrella of the Ravidassia identity.

Ravidas Jayanti mela at Varanasi

In Varanasi, while the NRIs and their families occupy the high-end hotels, ordinary pilgrims head towards the tented accommodation set up near an open field adjacent to the Guru Ravidas Janam Asthan Mandir.

Varanasi has been a popular pilgrimage destination for long time, but with the growing importance of Guru Ravidas Janam Asthan, January and February have become important to Varanasi locals as well.

The place begins to take on a festive atmosphere well before the birth anniversary of Guru Ravidas. Vendors of all kinds—sweets, toys, herbal medicines and more—set up shop near the mandir as hordes of devotees descend on the city. A particularly distinct presence among the shops are those selling books on Ambedkar, Jotiba Phule, Periyar and other reformers and leaders of the subaltern castes, including Mayawati and

Kanshi Ram. These shops also stock literature and posters of the dera sants, as well as books on the life and teachings of Guru Ravidas. Books on Kabir, Valmiki and other sants are also on display.

As I watched, I saw a teenage boy arguing with his mother for a book on Ambedkar that seemed expensive. In that moment, I could sense the profound impact that the Dera Ballan's Varanasi project has had beyond Punjab.

Over the years, the number of Ravidassias visitors have grown exponentially as awareness about the Guru Ravidas Janam Asthan has spread far and wide. The widespread use of mobile phones and social media has further expanded the networks of people, signs and symbols. The dera has clearly emerged as the centre of these networks beyond Punjab.

The huge makeshift kind of a township that emerges full of tent houses next to the mandir, with large flex banners of various states of India prominently displayed, is a telling testimony on the extent to which the movement has spread. From Kashmir to Karnataka and from Bihar to Uttarakhand, people from numerous states congregate at the Janam Asthan. Old and young, men and women meet, interact and exchange experiences, addresses and mobile numbers. It is from here that the consciousness of Ravidassia identity and its associated symbols spread to hundreds and thousands of villages and towns.

It is evident that some people initially associated with Dera Ballan on their own before becoming active leaders in their states or regions, ultimately bringing the sangat to this annual religious congregation. Kameshwar Das Ji Maharaj from Bihar, for instance, who now leads the Bihar sangat to these congregations, was first introduced to the Dera Ballan sants some years ago. He gradually became active in Patna and other cities and towns of Bihar, where the Ravidassia identity is not as strong.

An old woman from Chandauli, a nearby small town in Uttar Pradesh, summarized her experience to me in these words: 'I have come to Varanasi many times in my life, but used to wander around. Little did I know that our own guru's abode was right here! That our roots are here (*hamaar jadd to yahan hai*). Now I come here regularly as I feel like I am coming home, to our own people, to our own devta.'

The sentiment she expressed resonated with the dominant feeling among the pilgrims staying in the tented accomodations. Ravidas Jayanti has provided them with a sense of belonging and of an equal world, even if for just a few days—a feeling that they are deprived of in their everyday lives.

The longing for an equal world was palpable. Conversations with Ravidassias from Uttar Pradesh and Bihar illuminated the differences in the way the two regions—Punjab and Uttar Pradesh—have evolved socially, politically and culturally.

For instance, the lower economic profile of devotees from the Hindi heartland was clearly reflected in their lack of confidence and limited political expression. They were cautious and fearful in speaking about their marginalized lives. In contrast, Punjabi youth from similar caste-community backgrounds were full of descriptions of their autonomy and quest for justice, while the youth from the Hindi heartland lacked that sense of identity and pride in both individual and community existence.

During my visit to Varanasi in 2017, I met a person from a nearby town who was in his mid-forties and was selling booklets of poems he had written in praise of Guru Ravidas. As I stopped to buy a copy and to converse, I took pictures of him. The moment he saw me doing so, he asked anxiously, '*Babu, kahe hamra photo le rahe hain, kachhu galti ho gayi kaa?'* (Sir, why are you taking pictures of me? Have I done something wrong?) It was my turn to be unsettled by this response.

As I reassured him and dispelled his fears, he seemed calmer and shared his life story with me, including how he had begun writing poetry. That the poet had thought his act to be potentially 'illegal' speaks volumes about the scars that centuries of leading a subjugated, stifled life can wreak on one's psyche. This encounter left me numb and deeply pained.

To collect my thoughts, I sat down at a nearby tea stall, ordered a cup of tea and read through his poems. They primarily focused on the lives of Guru Ravidas and Ambedkar, urging Dalits to draw inspiration from these figures and cast off the yoke of traditions that had never treated them equally. A few poems were also dedicated to Mayawati, Jagjivan Ram and Kanshi Ram.

Babu Ram Gautam, the poet, belonged to Barabanki, Uttar Pradesh. His booklet, a collection of devotional poems titled *Guru Ravidas ke Anmol Bhajan* (*Precious Bhajans of Guru Ravidas*), contained about fifty pages.[2] Here are a few samples from the book:

Ai mere mitra abki kasi chalo
Yahan thagwan ka koi Sahara nahi
Guru Ravidas ki tum sharan me chalo
Unke charnan shish jhukate chalo.
Ab na panda pujarin ke bas jao nahi.
Apne devo ke dar pe tum jaate nahi,
Unke charnan me tum shish jhukaate nahi
Kahte Baburam daliton se kar jori ke
Dharam neeche Kisi se hamara nahi.
O my friend!

Here, there are no saviours to the cheated,
So come to the feet of Guru Ravidas.
Bow your head to him.
No need to go to any priest anymore
You don't seek your own Gods,
Nor do you bow your head to him.
Please listen to me, your Baburam,
I appeal to you my Dalit brethren
Our Dharam is no way inferior to others.

Tum kahe Baba Bhim ke Bhulawat hau
Baba sahib kanoon banain
Sabko barabar adhikaar debaine,
Tabhe se mauz uthawat ho
Tum kahe Baba Bhim ke Bhulawat hau.
Sahib Hammar begari chhodaine
Sab Dalitan ke upar uthaine,
Unhu kahe visrawat ho
Tum kahe Baba Bhim ke Bhulawat hau.
Bhaia hamare kuchch karo bichari
Baburam ki arzi bhari.
Why do you forget Baba Bhim?
He made the Constitution
Got everyone equality,
So you enjoy and have fun.
Why do you forget Baba Bhim then?
He got us out of forced labour
And uplifted us Dalits,
Why do you then forget Baba Bhim?
O brothers, please listen to me,
Your Baburam pleads with heavy heart.

Seer Gaovardhanpur at Varanasi on the occasion of Ravidas Jayanti thus offers a collage of multiple narratives and shades of Ravidassia movement from across various states, and not just Punjab. Punjab dera perhaps creates the fulcrum around which these narratives, sometimes coalescing and at other times competing, get to converge together at one place.

Baba Gheda: A parallel narrative and counterpoint

The name Banta Ram Gheda or Baba Gheda, depending on which side of the narrative one is, and stories about him and his contribution to the making of the Guru Ravidas Janam Asthan in Seer Goverdhanpur evoke an uncomfortable silence among the Dera Ballan functionaries.

However, the narrative, even as a marginal subtext, still survives and indicates the initial struggle for power and appropriation. In other words, not everything related to the Janam Asthan is uncontested and trouble-free.

There are parallel narratives questioning the legitimacy of Dera Ballan's claim that the temple marks Guru Ravidas' birthplace. There are people and voices right in the middle of the dingy lane that connects the Janam Asthan Mandir to the boundary wall of the BHU campus who espouse counter claims and a different history.

Banta Ram Gheda was from the Santokhpura area in Jalandhar. He was a railway employee in Delhi and served as the president of the union of Scheduled Caste and Scheduled Tribe employees. He was initially associated with Dera Ballan and was a devout follower of both Guru Ravidas and Sant Sarwan Das. He harboured a dream of establishing an independent identity for the community, to the extent that he proposed a separate book containing only the shabads of Guru Ravidas, even during the days when the dera had a more syncretic ethos and followed the rahit of the Guru Granth Sahib.

Being a devout follower, he made it his mission to work for the Guru Ravidas Janam Asthan in Varanasi. As a railway employee, it was easy for him to travel to Varanasi frequently and mobilize local resources and people from his community to support the mission.

'He actually did all the spadework in the initial years,' an old dera follower, who had witnessed the rise of Dera Ballan and its Varanasi project from close quarters, conceded. 'But with time, as the dera took full control of the site, and later with the formation of the Shri Guru Ravidas Janam Asthan Public Charitable Trust, Banta Ram Gheda was pushed into the background. He eventually shifted his base to Khuralgarh.'

However, there are still some who remember him. One of them is Mahant Acharya Bharat Bhushan Das, the national president of Guru Ravidas Janam Asthan Sodh Evam Seva Sansthan Nyas, Varanasi. He works under the umbrella organization All India Adi-Dharma Mission. Mahant Bharat Bhushan, a local resident of Varanasi, is an articulate man in his mid-forties. He is one of the main proponents of the parallel narrative that questions the 'monopoly' of Dera Ballan over the Ravidas Janam Asthan. Bharat Bhushan is the head mahant of a temple adjacent to the Shri Guru Ravidas Janam Asthan Mandir. A large statue of Ravidas stands in front of the temple-cum-residence of the mahant, whose followers are largely drawn from nearby villages and towns in Uttar Pradesh. He believes that he represents the 'local' perspective of the Ravidas movement concerning the guru's birthplace. In his view, the site of his residence and the temple within it is the actual birthplace.

Bharat Bhushan's perspective presents Guru Ravidas within the *saguni* tradition, meaning the tradition emphasizing devotional practices and worship of deities with forms, and within the broader Hindu cosmology. This is also probably because Ravidas himself comes from Varanasi and is said to have been a disciple of Ramanand. More importantly, Bharat Bhushan seemed to have a 'son of the soil'-centric world view regarding Guru Ravidas, which gives him a sense of cultural 'ownership' over the spiritual legacy of Guru Ravidas. Much of his discomfort and conflict emanates from what he calls the 'Punjabi appropriation of Guru Ravidas'. He was particularly vitriolic about Sant Garib Das, the fourth chief mahant of Dera Ballan, whom he believed isolated the Janam Asthan from its local roots, making it an exclusive extension of Dera Ballan.

Bharat Bhushan's residence, a modest two-storey house, has been dwarfed by the magnificent, multi-storey Shri Guru Ravidas Janam Asthan Mandir, which is topped by gold-plated domes. Its recognition by the Uttar Pradesh government as a heritage site settled any dispute in favour of the Dera Ballan-managed trust. Bharat Bhushan believes this is the result of the dera's Kanshi Ram connection.

Manyavar Kanshi Ram, founder of the Bahujan Samaj Party (BSP), was from the Doaba region of Punjab and belonged to the same caste-community that Dera Ballan identified with. With the rise of the BSP in Uttar Pradesh and the ascendance of Mayawati, Kanshi Ram's protégé, as chief minister on four occasions—and her influence as a formidable political force—Dera Ballan seized the opportunity to consolidate its roots in Varanasi.

During the building of the mandir at Seer Goverdhanpur, the dera was able to attract prominent dignitaries, including President K.R. Naraynan, Kanshi Ram, Kalyan Singh, Mayawati and others, for key milstones at the site.

Bharat Bhushan, in his attempt to portray Dera Ballan as opportunististic and unethical, cites the instance of Banta Singh Gheda and how the dera functionaries and management not only sidelined him but also discounted his contributions.*

On every Ravidas Jayanti, Bharat Bhushan's organization also decorates his premises—the 'original' birthplace as he claims—and organizes langar and other activities. However, the long, serpentine queues of thousands of devotees that assemble on the birth anniversary—stretching from the BHU campus towards the Janam Asthan Mandir from pre-dawn—do not visit Bharat Bhushan's abode. Few bother to look that way, as most have eyes only for the magnificent and glittering gold-plated domes of the Dera Ballan mandir. Nonetheless, some devotees, particularly from states like Andhra Pradesh, Telangana and Maharashtra, who do not understand much of the local politics, do visit Bharat Bhushan's site as well.

Bharat Bhushan is an educated man with a master's degree, a Bachelor of Education and a degree in library science. His companions include sadhus of various backgrounds, mostly from nearby regions, all standing in solidarity with him. The upper storey of his house has a library where books on Mira, Ravidas, Kabir, Valmiki and the Arya Samaj are neatly kept, along with a book on the Vishwa Hindu Parishad's Ashok Singhal.

Much before the Ravidas Janam Asthan Mandir became a popular pilgrimage destination, Varanasi had only a few small sites commemorating the legacy and legends of Guru Ravidas. One of these is the Guru Ravidas temple and memorial complex at Rajghat on the river Ganga. This is believed to be the site where Guru Ravidas performed the legendary miracle of making

---

* Meeting with Bharat Bhushan on 9 February 2017 for the first time at his ashram in Seer Govardhanpur, Varanasi.

a stone float on the Ganga in front of the king and the Brahmin priests who had challenged his sacred power. The temple was constructed with the support and initiative of Babu Jagjivan Ram, the Congress politician who later switched allegiance to the Janata Party and served as deputy prime minister in its 1977-79 government. He laid the foundation of the temple in April 1971. Today, his daughter Meira Kumar, a prominent Congress leader, oversees its upkeep and maintenance through the Ravidas Smarak Trust based in Delhi.

One gets the sense that the smaller sites are largely symbolic, mostly unattended through the year except during the visit of a dignitary or community leader or on Ravidas Jayanti. Interestingly, many devotees from Punjab and other states who throng the city to attend the Ravidas Jayanti celebrations at the Janam Asthan now also visit these smaller sites. The Guru Ravidas temple has, over the decades, become larger and more grand. In 2005, Meira Kumar began the tradition of a daily Ganga aarti, or lighting a lamp at the ghat, perhaps inspired by the popular ritual at the Kashi Vishwanath complex. It is clear that these smaller sites, unlike the Dera Ballan initiative, are more anchored in Hindu tradition and cosmology, aiming to coexist as subsidiary offshoots to the mainstream. During one of my visits to the ghat and the complex on the eve of Ravidas Jayanti, I met Bharat Bhushan and his companions, who were planning the activities for the following day's event, while Meira Kumar had arrived to oversee the anniversary event at the mandir complex.

This ghat is quite far from the Kashi Vishwanath ghat and temple, considered to be the heart of Varanasi according to Hindu tradition. It is believed that the temple is located at the tip of Lord Shiva's trishul, or trident, and is the gateway to heaven for those who breathe their last here. Adjacent to the

Guru Ravidas temple complex is an eclectic shrine dedicated to Bhaisasur and Shayar Mata, who are worshipped by the *Nishaads,* the community who traditionally worked in water-related occupations such as fishing, boating etc. of the region as they believe them to be their *ishta dev* and *devi* (a worshipper's personal deity in the Hindu tradition). This temple too retains its connections with Hindu motifs and symbols, as pictures of Hindu gods and goddesses adorn its walls and tridents are placed alongside the main deities.

The Dera Ballan movement and its pilgrimage project in Varanasi, prominently and consciously foregrounding Guru Ravidas in a *nirakaar, nirguni* form, traditions that believed in the formless idea of gods and goddesses, shaped by the sacred cultural sensibilities of Punjab, clearly strives for an alternative vision of Kashi. While a calendar image of Ravidas created in Uttar Pradesh might incorporate symbols of saguni and Vaishanavite Hindu traditions, the pictures, posters and other representations of Guru Ravidas in Punjab and at Dera Ballan will have none of these. Dera Ballan has adopted 'Hari' as their symbol, as they believe it signifies the formless *adi shakti,* or eternal universal power—a view contested by many others in Varanasi, such as Bharat Bhushan. He argues, 'Guru Ravidas used the words Govind, Madhav, Prabhu Ram but never Hari in his shlokas and shabads.' He believes the word 'Soham', used by the Ad-Dharmi movement, is the appropriate symbol.

Dera Ballan's literature, images, books, pamphlets and other publicity materials mostly distance themselves from both Hindu and Sikh symbolism, instead charting an independent path. However, Dera Ballan generously uses images of Ambedkar. The dera and its followers take immense pride in his legacy. From its library to rest houses in Ballan and other locations, such as hospitals and dharamshalas, pictures of Ambedkar adorn the walls. Music videos, songs and pamphlets of Dera Ballan almost always feature images of dera sants alongside Ambedkar, integrating Ambedkar into its religious iconography. This reflects the dera's political orientation—while Guru Ravidas is its sacred icon, Ambedkar is regarded as its political guru. Most popular songs about Dera Ballan speak about Ambedkar's contribution to the community, with frequent references to his role as the chief architect of India's Constitution.

In a way, Ambedkar provides the Ravidassia movement—which is critiqued by its detractors for promoting a particular sant tradition and therefore undermining the larger Dalit consolidation—with a national framework. This turn towards Ambedkar, which Dera Ballan took from the mid 1980s onwards, interestingly coincided with the rise of Bahujan politics and the ascendance of Kanshi Ram, who hailed from the Doaba region of Punjab.

The rise of Ambedkar as a prominent figure in that politics, which had national appeal, aligned well with the independent path that the Dera Ballan leaders were exploring as they moved beyond the Ad-Dharmi label that they had carried for so long.

The Janam Asthan project at Varanasi has emerged as a grand billboard showcasing Dera Ballan's aspirations to the world. From a small cluster of huts in a nondescript village in Punjab at the beginning of the last century to its reach and stature today—the story of Dera Ballan is phenomenal. By the late 1990s, with the rise of what sociologist Manuel Castells called the 'Network Society', and as the world became increasingly interconnected, Dera Ballan too came of age, becoming an active anchor in mediating not only between local nodes, but also between the local and global, in pursuit of its mission to forge a global Ravidassia identity. The significance of the Varanasi pilgrimage lies in its potential to serve as a global platform for a new Ravidassia identity. Varanasi brings Ballan closer to Badayun and Wolverhampton; it creates a confluence between the nirguni and saguni, the rich and the poor, ultimately fostering a parallel universe of the subalterns. For the Ravidassia, Varanasi is, therefore, a utopia, a Begumpura experiment in real time.

6

Myth of a Monolith: The Ravidassia Identity and Its Reality

The articulation of the Ravidassia identity in Punjab, as expressed through Dera Ballan and its fractured trajectory, especially since 2009, resonates with the chequered history of larger Dalit politics in the region and adds to the complications surrounding it. If numbers matter in a democracy, then how does one explain the near-total absence of Dalit politics in Punjab—a state with the highest Scheduled Caste (SCs) population in the country, estimated at 32 per cent even by conservative measures? Adding to the puzzle is that, besides numerical strength, there is a substantial diaspora support base, and the region boasts a formidable line-up of homegrown revolutionary Dalit leaders, such as Babu Mangoo Ram, Kanshi Ram and others.

The Doaba region of Punjab, especially around Jalandhar City, has always had a high level of social awareness on issues of identity politics and discrimination, largely due to the community's strong economic standing through the leather business. Ambedkar visited this area in 1952, after resigning as law minister, and had a huge following in the Boota Mandi locality, including among some prominent business families of the region. Many of Ambedkar's associates during his time in Delhi from the late 1940s till his death in 1956 were from this area.

There are standard explanations for this situation, the most prominent being the dominance of landed communities, primarily Jatt Sikhs and a few other castes. It is argued that this dominance prevented the Dalit community from charting its own independent political journey. Instead, they expressed themselves through the Shiromani Akali Dal (SAD) or the Indian National Congress (INC), the two main political parties in the state, again largely led by Jatts. The BSP, perceived as the face of Dalit politics, has been reduced to a footnote in Punjab politics, with its vote share falling from 16 per cent to 4 per cent, and now to less than 2 per cent over the last two decades.* Economic and materialist explanations aside, the role of religious identity and the politics surrounding it in determining the status of local Dalit politics has been either underplayed or inadequately addressed. Recently, the mushrooming of deras in the region as sites of Dalit consolidation and the propagation of Ambedkar's ideology has once again brought religion into focus.

---

* In 1992, it secured 16 per cent of the vote in Punjab, but it dropped to 4 per cent in the 2012 assembly polls, and in the 2022 assembly polls, it further dipped to 1.77 per cent.

Vikas Vasudeva, 'In Punjab, BSP's "chronic spoilsport" role continues to shrink, yet it may be spoilsport on handful seats', *The Hindu*, 17 May 2024, https://www.thehindu.com/elections/lok-sabha/in-punjab-bsps-chronic-spoilsport-role-continues-to-shrink-yet-it-may-be-spoilsport-on-handful-seats/article68185536.ece

Three local narratives[1]

An important point to remember is that while democracy may be about numbers, people and cultures are not. There is enough work on the census, its politics of enumeration, and how it has misinformed and misled, failing to capture the fuzziness of our world—especially its caste-ridden religious landscape—since its inception as a colonial tool in mid-nineteenth-century India.[2]

Even today, in Punjab, the oft-cited figure of '32 per cent SC population' fails to provide any insight into the marginalization of Dalit politics in the state. In the absence of in-depth sociological fieldwork among the people of contemporary Punjab, numbers serve as mere props for standard, almost clichéd answers to questions that clearly need a more nuanced, ground-level analysis. For example, several pertinent questions remain unresolved: Do deras divide or unite? Why has the Doaba region, despite its intellectual and material resources, not provided leadership to Dalit politics in Punjab? How does one unravel the paradox of Ambedkar's immense popularity, yet the limited acceptance of his prescription of Buddhism as a model in Punjab? Did the local ideologues and leaders based in Doaba ignore their poorer cousins in the Malwa and Majha regions and instead focus on overseas bases?

Questions such as these arise repeatedly when one visits the region and meets both prominent and lesser-known individuals, especially the old-timers, in the villages and towns.

Based on over a decade of fieldwork in the region—largely around Jalandhar and among the Ravidassias in the Doaba region, but also in other parts—three significant local narratives emerge. All three originate from the broader Ravidassia caste cluster, yet are ideologically and spatially distinct. These narratives highlight the critical role that religion plays in the region and shed light on the complex dynamics that its interaction with politics unleashes locally.

These perspectives, through the ethnographic profiles of three distinct intellectuals, bring forth and highlight the nuances within the perceived monolith and its associated simplification.

Dera Ballan has been at the forefront of the tussle to appropriate the Ad-Dharmi legacy and replace it with the Ravidassia identity. However, it has not been an easy journey. Regional, ideological and political imbalances have led to varied responses to the idea of a standardized template for Dalits in the region.

The discomfort felt by other Scheduled Caste groups—such as the Valmikis, Kabir panthis and others—with the idea of a particular tradition being imposed upon them, which is seen as a sign of dominance and arrogance, is quite evident on the ground.

These three perspectives further underline the myth of a monolithic Ravidassia identity, even among the Ravidassias themselves.

L.R. Balley: A Buddhist-Ambedkarite*[3]

Mr L.R. Balley, aged eighty-eight, a prominent Dalit thinker and ideologue of the region, lives in Jalandhar town. He met Dr B.R. Ambedkar for the last time on 30 September 1956, in Delhi. Finding Baba Saheb critically ill, Balley pledged that he will serve the Ambedkar Mission to the last drop of his blood.

---

* L.R. Balley passed away on 6 July 2023.

On the day of Baba Sahib's death—6 December 1956—he resigned from his permanent central government job and dedicated his life to the actvities of the Ambedkar Mission. He has been the editor of *Bhim Patrika* since 1958 and a founding trustee of the Ambedkar Bhawan in Jalandhar.

A voracious reader and writer, Balley has written more than a hundred books in English, Hindi, Punjabi, Urdu and Marathi, in addition to translating Ambedkar's works into these languages. As an activist-thinker, he has visited Canada, the USA, the UK, Germany, France, Australia, the Philippines, Taiwan, Afghanistan, Pakistan, Thailand, China and Malaysia, leading to the establishment of Buddha vihars and Ambedkar centres in some of these countries.

Two large, elegantly framed portraits—one of Buddha and the other of Ambedkar—alongside huge wooden almirahs brimming with books by and about Ambedkar, greet visitors in L.R. Balley's drawing room.

As we settled into our sofas, sipping hot tea on a wintry morning, L.R. Balley nostalgically recounted stories from his youth and his first meeting with Ambedkar in Delhi. After numerous failed attempts to meet his idol, he finally succeeded with the help of a fellow Punjabi man known to Ambedkar. He met Baba Saheb one morning when the iconic leader was out for a walk.

L.R. Balley recalled how Dr Savita Ambedkar, Baba Sahib's wife, would often misinform visitors—perhaps to prevent the ailing leader from overexerting himself with too many interactions—saying that he was not home, asleep or unwell whenever Balley and others tried to meet him.

The conversation was full of rich anecdotes and insights about Ambedkar's final years, as well as Mr Balley's own foray into Ambedkarite politics.

L.R. Balley was involved in Dalit politics through the Scheduled Caste Federation and the Republican Party of India (RPI). In addition to his work with the Ambedkar Mission, *Bhim Patrika* publications and his own reading and writing on Ambedkar, he unsuccessfully contested two parliamentary elections—first in 1962 and then in 1967—as well as two assembly elections between 1970 and 1980. He attributed his electoral failures to the communal Hindu politics of the time, which spread the canard that he ate beef. 'The fact that I, as a true Ambedkarite, always sided with the progressive forces and never had any truck with religious or communal politics went against me. But I do not care,' he said.

He remained a committed Buddhist, steadfastly following his idol's model of religious conversion. Given that the Buddhist model did not quite work in Punjab, he now reluctantly concedes that there may have been some merit in the view that Ambedkar's prescription of Buddhism as a pan-Indian framework was too monolithic for the diverse social and religio-cultural realities of Dalit life and did not strike a chord with local sensibilities. However, at a personal level, there has been no weakening of his commitment to Buddhism.

As a political strategy, Balley reluctantly acknowledges that there may have been a disconnect. He dismisses the movement for a new religion around the Ravidassia identity led by Dera Ballan. He believes that the movement has divided the Dalit community and argues that, since Guru Ravidas did not propose any religious framework, there is no merit in establishing a new religion in his name.

It is clear that L.R. Balley does not appreciate the dera-based movements that have sprung up in every nook and corner of the region. He remains a die-hard follower of Ambedkar's prescription of a non-ritualized, pragmatic form of Buddhism as the ideal model for Dalits to follow for a broader and more stable consolidation of Dalit identity.

Despite the fact that the number of people who converted to Buddhism in the region remains negligible, and the project never truly took off, and despite the progressive decline in the popularity of *Bhim Patrika*, L.R. Balley remains steadfast in his commitment to the pledge he made to his mentor, Baba Saheb Ambedkar.

Manohar Lal Mahey: A Ravidassia-Ambedkarite

Manohar Lal Mahey, aged sixty-eight, is a prominent businessman from the Boota Mandi area of Jalandhar. He is the grandson of Seth Sundar Das, who donated Rs 11,000—a princely sum in those days—on behalf of his community to Ambedkar during the latter's visit to Boota Mandi for a public event in 1952.

Like others in the Boota Mandi area, Manohar Lal was interested in higher studies, and Ambedkar's work was a constant source of inspiration for him. He earned a postgraduate degree in political science and later joined a bank as an officer, but his engagement with academic pursuits and activities related to Ambedkar continued. He also assisted anthropologist Professor Mark Juergensmeyer from Berkeley, USA, during his fieldwork on the dera phenomenon in the area in the 1970s.

Manohar Lal has been an active supporter of broader Dalit community consolidation. As the secretary of the Dera Ballan Trust for the Guru Ravidas Janam Asthan from 1984 to 1992, he is deeply concerned by the politics surrounding Dera Ballan and the internal squabbling and splintering.

Unlike L.R. Balley, however, he foregrounds his Ravidassia identity and actively invests in it. He disagrees with L.R.

Balley, and argues, 'The reason L.R. Balley could not be successful politically is because he did not take into account local sentiments that were built around the Chamar identity and Guru Ravidas. Buddhism had no place here. The affluent community of Chamars of the region always revered their guru, besides many others.'

Like most of his community, he is a staunch follower of Baba Saheb Ambedkar. The drawing room of his palatial house is adorned with portraits of Baba Saheb, while the upper façade of the house prominently features 'Har', the Ravidassia symbol, inscribed in marble. What emerges is a seamless merging of these two identities—Ravidassia and Ambedkarite.

Manohar Lal Mahey explains: 'Why should there be any confusion? Like other contemporary Bhakti poets and saints, Guru Ravidas was as revered. It is true Baba Saheb advocated Buddhism, but one has to be flexible enough to accommodate and rework his prescriptions, including the model of religious conversion to Buddhism. His larger messages on education and struggle are far more important for us than anything else. He is our political guru, but Guru Ravidas is our spiritual guru. Why look elsewhere when we have one of our own to guide us spiritually?'

Manohar Lal emphasizes the importance of community unity and values coexistence over confrontation as a strategy. When the Vienna incident occurred in 2009, he actively worked on the ground to calm the inflamed sentiments of his community. However, when Dera Ballan and its leadership later aggressively pursued a separatist path, Manohar Lal did not approve and distanced himself from their activities. He explains: 'Our community, whether in business or not, is part of local inter-dependent economic networks and hence to talk of a combative and independent path is strategically a mistake.'

To introduce his world view, Manohar Lal Mahey shows me the puja ghar (small worship place) in his house. At the centre is a statue of Guru Ravidas, surrounded by smaller statues of Shirdi Sai Baba, Goddess Lakshmi, Saraswati, Guru Nanak and the saints of Dera Ballan, among others.

Manohar Lal Mahey never had political aspirations. He resigned from his bank job to pursue his own export-import leather business and has travelled extensively around the world. Half of his family lives in Canada and other overseas locations. Mahey, however, remains active through his organization, Vigilant Brotherhood (International) Jalandhar, keeping his activism alive by organizing conferences and seminars in the city and other places.

Paramjit Singh Kainth: A Sikh-Ambedkarite

Paramjit Singh Kainth comes from Patiala, in the Malwa region. At fifty-four, he is much younger than L.R. Balley and Manohar Lal Mahey. He contested the state assembly elections thrice on a BSP ticket—in 1992, 1997 and 2007—losing on all three occasions. He began his political journey as a close associate of Babu Kanshi Ram, the iconic BSP founder and leader.

Paramjit Singh Kainth recalls his time with Kanshi Ram in Punjab, organizing rallies to which both he and his mentor rode cycles. He comes across as a simple man with an easy demeanour, yet he holds an aggressive, uncompromising political stance focused on creating a united Dalit front based on grassroots issues such as land, employment, education and health, rather than on religion or faith, which he believes distract from the movement's real goals.

Paramjit Singh is the president of the National Scheduled Caste Alliance (NSCA) in Punjab, and according to his visiting card, he is also the president of the Chamar Mahan Sabha (Grand Alliance of the Chamars). The card prominently states, '*Garv se kaho Ham Chamar Hain*' (announce with pride that you belong to the Chamar community).

Paramjit Singh is bitter about how religion has hijacked the agenda, causing the more pragmatic priorities of Dalit politics in the state to be abandoned. He blames Gurmeet Ram Rahim Singh of Dera Sacha Sauda for one of his electoral defeats.

He believes the deras exploit people and politics for their own narrow interests, lacking any positive agenda and only serving to divide the community.

On the contribution of ideologues and leaders from the Doaba region, he minces no words: 'What is their contribution to Dalit politics, other than writing books and collaborating with the rich diaspora settled in Canada, USA and UK? Doaba Dalits could have used their affluence in unifying the people from the other less privileged regions of Majha and Malwa in Punjab, but they never really bothered. They could reach Edmonton, but not Patiala.'

Paramjit Singh dismisses the Ravidassia movement at Ballan, believing that the Guru Granth Sahib as a holy text represents everyone, and hence to talk of a new religion or book is meaningless. A turbaned man, Paramjit Singh respects all cultural sentiments yet remains firmly rooted in the materialist and pragmatic framework of Baba Saheb Ambedkar. He respects the Guru Granth Sahib, and his fight, as he puts it, is against 'Jattism'—the way the Jatts have 'occupied' Sikhism. He further explains, 'Sikhism is a great religion, and there is nothing wrong with the religion. Rather, the gurus honour people of all faiths and castes. The Guru Granth Sahib includes banis or hymns of people and saints from other castes and religions such as Ravidas, Kabir and Baba Farid . . . We are not against anyone but for humanism.'

He now aims to launch a social movement across Punjab to highlight the real issues facing Dalits in the state. When asked, 'Why did you lose all the elections you contested?' he responds with a smile, his face betraying no other emotion, and says, 'So what, even Baba Saheb Ambedkar never won an election.'

Paramjit Singh Kainth comes across as a person of steely resolve and with a clear plan.

Ambedkar as a constant

The prominence of the deras and the identity articulation around Guru Ravidas in the Doaba region is evident. What is remarkable, however, is the emergence of Baba Saheb Ambedkar as a constant presence in all these deras—not only in Dera Ballan, but also in others that are not necessarily of the 'activist' type.

The Sant Baba Phool Nath Dera, for instance, has huge portraits of Ambedkar on its premises. Interestingly, these deras reflect not just ordinary existential anxieties, such as the dream of an overseas job—typical of the region and symbolized by offerings of toy planes to deities—but also an aspiration for a larger, interconncted collective shaped by narratives drawn from Ambedkar's life stories and legends of Guru Ravidas and other saints. For example, one of the paintings at Baba Phool Nath Dera depicts Ravidas, Valmiki and Kabir walking alongside the Buddha, followed by Ambedkar and his band of followers. These images give expression to the community's collective desire for a grand alliance that subsumes all fissiparous narratives and ideologies within the community.

The rise of Ambedkar as a constant figure among Dalits across the state and region symbolizes a growing political awareness, especially among the youth. While religious affiliations vary from region to region, Ambedkar remains a unifying presence.

The three narratives discussed above illustrate the fractured nature of Dalit narratives, highlighting the limitations of a monolithic discourse centred on any particular religious identity, including Ravidassia. Given the significance of religion in people's lives, what seems important is not to undermine the space of any imagination, but rather to develop strategies to unify through the glue provided by Ambedkar.

There is no doubt that there is overwhelming support for the Ravidassia identity (rather than Ad-Dharmi), especially in the Doaba region, though the intensity diminishes as one moves towards regions like Malwa. In fact, even in Jalandhar, support for the Ravidassia identity does not necessarily mean the exclusion of other traditions, as we saw in the case of Manohar Lal Mahey.

Similarly, Paramjit Singh Kainth does not dismiss Guru Ravidas; rather, he emphasizes his Chamar identity, just as people in Doaba enjoy and enthusiastically dance to Ginni Mahi's *Danger Chamar* songs (see the following chapter for more details). However, he sees no value in the Dera Ballan-led movement for a separate religious identity, as he believes this only hinders the struggle for a united Dalit political front in the state.

Another significant point is that, unlike L.R. Balley and Manohar Lal Mahey—both from Doaba—Paramjit Singh Kainth is from the Malwa belt.

There is a general perception in some of Punjab's poorer pockets that ideologues and Ambedkar Mission activists have focused more on their wealthy NRI bases in the West rather than expanding their activities in the regions beyond Doaba.

The broader point is that the discriminatory, caste-based practices within Sikhism, contrary to its tenets, have led to the mushrooming of separate gurudwaras and deras of all hues and inclinations, often marred by petty internal power struggles. However, this shared experience of injustice and discrimination could possibly serve as the catalyst for a larger movement towards a more equitable society, provided that Dalit leaders and ideologues in the state look beyond their silos.

It is evident that religion plays a critical role in the region, creating multiple axes of alliances and rifts that, interestingly, have regional and class-based dimensions. As Paramjit Singh points out, Malwa and Majha will have different perspectives compared to Doaba. However, even within Doaba, L.R. Balley and Manohar Lal Mahey, despite coming from the same region, hold opposing views and perspectives on Dalit politics and its future path in Punjab.

It is not without reason that Ambedkar underlined the significance of religion in our society. He understood that caste drew its sustenance from Hinduism, and he sought to replace that framework in the quest for a better, more equitable world—hence his decision to convert to Buddhism. However, Buddhism was only a means—the goal was a casteless society. Dalit politics in Punjab must understand this, and in doing so, its stakeholders need to be sensitive to the nuances of local religious traditions and their diversity.

What tilts the mood in favour of optimism is the omnipresence of Ambedkar's portraits and even libraries dedicated to his writings and those of Dalit scholars in deras and Ravidassia gurudwaras. The new Dalit leadership will have to build on this constant and navigate the maze of religious formations with sensitivity and care. In short, religion will remain relevant from whichever angle one approaches Punjab politics. This is especially true when aspiring to establish a consolidated Dalit political presence in the state.

The near-total rejection of Buddhism in Punjab highights the dangers of imposing a standardized model that undermines local cultural sensibilities and socio-political history.

The Channi experiment and its fate as a signifier

The 2022 assembly elections in Punjab and the near-total wipeout of the reigning Congress at the hustings, under the leadership of Charanjit Singh Channi—a Ramdassia Dalit—as the chief ministerial candidate, once again brought the focus on the future of Dalit politics in Punjab.

Channi had become the chief minister in September 2021, a position he held until March 2022, when the assembly elections took place. The Congress' decision to announce a Dalit as their chief ministerial candidate in a state with the highest SC population in the country, but with almost no political clout, was seen by many as a masterstroke. However, the election results turned out to be a damp squib.

Many factors contributed to the downfall of the Congress, but the fact that Charanjit Singh Channi lost both seats he contested generated serious debate about the future of Dalits in Punjab politics, especially regarding the possibility of a Dalit chief minister in a state historically dominated by the influential Jatt Sikhs.

The only other person from the lower order of the caste pyramid to become chief minister of Punjab was Giani Zail Singh, who belonged to an artisanal caste called the Ramgarhia. He later went on to become the President of India. Most of Punjab's other chief ministers have been from the Jatt Sikh community.

A significant reason behind the failure of the Channi experiment in Punjab is the fractured history of the Dalits. It appears that Channi and the Congress were carried away by the mistaken belief that Dalits form a monolithic group.

Many observers and local analysts believe that Channi's overemphasis on his Dalit identity—especially his repeated visits to Dera Ballan and his championing of the Ravidassia identity before the elections—did two things. First, it riled up the Jatt Sikhs and unsettled their entrenched power structures, pushing them away from the Congress and towards the Aam Aadmi Party (AAP). Second, other Dalit caste groups felt excluded and marginalized.

It is worth noting that Channi announced many schemes and inaugurated ambitious multi-crore projects during his visits to Dera Ballan, including a centre dedicated to the study of Ravidas Bani. One such visit was on the eve of Republic Day, when he chose to spend the night at Dera Ballan instead of following protocol and staying at the government guest house.

Of course, the internal squabbling within the Congress and conflicting leadership messages also harmed the party's prospects. However, those who had placed high hopes on Channi's ascendance as a Dalit chief minister were left disillusioned and embarrassed, given the drubbing he and his party received in both constituencies where he contested and lost.

Both M.L. Mahey and Paramjit Kainth agree with this line of argument. Mahey considers it a 'setback' to Dalit politics in the region. With the BSP almost non-existent in the state, Mahey believes, 'The Dalits of the region will have to now think together and chalk out a combined road map for the future.'

He confessed that he had tried to advise those working with Channi not to overplay the Dera Ballan card, but to no avail. This aligns with Mahey's long-held view that Dera Ballan's aggressive push for a separate religion and holy book lacked support from the broader sadhu-sangat, and that the dera should have made efforts to bring others on board, initiating consensus-building measures.

Similarly, Paramjit Singh, who has always been dismissive of the dera culture—viewing them as nothing more than 'shops' under one sant or another—believes that Channi's disastrous performance in the election should be a wake-up call for the Dalits of the region.

He asserts that the only way the Dalit community can emerge as a powerful force is by channelling and mobilizing its resources around issues such as education, employment and representation in the public space. He believes that religion fragments the community and hinders its consolidation and solidarity.

He also suggsted that Channi had not previously been known for contributing to his community until the election, when he started openly showcasing his Dalit identity. Clearly, that approach did not strike a chord with the community.

Mythmaking happens in the present. However, sooner or later, myths are confronted by reality. Yet, myths carry the potential for fostering aspirations and anticipating emancipatory paths.

The reality of South Asian streams of religion and faith is that they represent enmeshment rather than clean linearity. Their foundations are intertwined, branching off into various congeries of faiths. The articulation of the Ravidassia identity also grapples with this fuzziness and the convoluted nature of the identity menu.

Any religious movement that attempts to carve out a distinct boundary necessitates the imagining of a myth. The Ravidassia identity is no exception.

7

Songs of Protest and the Politics of Posters: Decoding Popular Cultural Expressions

Visuals and songs arc powerful expressions of popular sentiments. While Punjab is known for its peppy beats and songs that have, over the years, come to command a huge pan-Indian fan following, the dominance of particular types of songs and music also underlines the asymmetry of power and the contested nature of the cultural milieu.

Hence, the emergence of a new wave of music clearly reflects the changing dynamics and reconstitution of the established order—or at least signals the existence of a countercurrent pushing towards an alternative.

The cultural terrain of the region is so politically sensitive that even posters, banners and pamphlets echo the broader mood. For instance, the power dynamics between various caste groups, as well as between different deras and sants, are reflected in the posters and banners displayed in towns and cities during anniversaries and significant political events. The appearance and disappearance of individuals from these posters and banners gives one a good sense of the internal churnings that are otherwise hard to discern.

The visual space is sensitive yet imbued with meaning. Pictures of Guru Ravidas, for instance, are presented differently in Punjab and Uttar Pradesh. In Punjab, especially in Dera Ballan's publicity materials, Guru Ravidas is shown mostly without a tilak on his forehead and without any symbols of Vaishanavite Hindu traditions, such as a wooden bead garland. Enter Uttar Pradesh, however, and things begin to change. Even the Janam Asthan at Seer Goverdhanpur is referred to as 'mandir' and not 'dera', and images of Guru Ravidas frequently include Vaishnavite symbols.

Songs of protest

The emergence of Dalit singers, or 'mission singers' as they are popularly called in the region, especially after the Vienna attack, reflects the growing chasm between the Jatt Sikhs and the Ravidassia community. Consider the titles of some of these videos and CDs: *Fighter Chamara*, *Putt Chamara da*, *Jago Ravidassia*, *Hummer* and *Sadda haq*. These songs and videos are provocative and often contain lyrics and visuals that challenge the hegemony of the Jatt Sikhs.

It is worth noting that, until recently, Dalits primarily played what is called 'Jatt pop music' in their vehicles, at weddings, parties and other events. Jatt pop music celebrates Jatt history and culture, paying scant attention to the heroes of other communities. These songs celebrate the hypermasculinity and the land-owning status of the Jatt Sikhs. The Punjabi pop industry is dominated by songs featuring the word 'Jatt' in their titles.

In this context, a song from Sunarah's album *Aarhab Chamara* (Stubborn Chamar) stands out as completely different. It seeks to revive the glorious past of the Chamar community by invoking the sacrifice of Jai Singh Khalkhat, a Chamar who was hanged by the Mughals for refusing to renounce Sikhism. The prominence given to this bit of history about Jai Singh clearly indicates that the Ravidassias have always been loyal to Sikhism; it is only due to the unequal treatment meted out to the community that they are now seeking freedom and autonomy. As one young man in Jalandhar said, 'Despite such supreme sacrifices of our people in Sikh history, they were unceremoniously ignored and Sikhism became a religion of Jatt Sikhs only.'

Unlike Sunarah's songs, many other songs and videos emerging from the Chamar community feature violent, hypermasculine content, with young men shown armed, riding SUVs and beating up opponents. These videos are extremely popular among the youth, as they perhaps match—or even surpass—the perceived macho image of the Jatts.

A quick look at the opening lines of some of the popular songs gives one a sense of how these singers are giving voice to issues of identity and caste assertion:

Hath leke hathiyar, Jad nikle Chamar
Phir vekheyo pataka, kiven payo mitro.
Aaj dekhde pana keda lao mitro

When Chamars walk out with their weapons in their hands,
Friends, watch out for the fireworks.
Then we shall see who crosses our path.

(From Pamma Sunarah's *Fighter Chamara*, 2011)

Kharka dharka karna kamm
Ravidassia da,
Aiven nahi hunde
Charche Chamara de

To create loud noises and ruffle feathers
Is what the followers of Ravidassia do,
It is not for nothing
That the Chamars are being discussed.

(From Roop Lal Dhir's *Hummer 2* album, 2012)

Some singers, like Roop Lal Dhir and S.S. Azad, were originally folk singers but have now become mission singers, claiming to sing for the community and its gurus rather than for money. Other popular singers include Kaler Kanth, Harbhajan Tajpuri, Miss Pooja and Rajni Thakarwal. The rise of mission singers after 2009 cannot be a mere coincidence; they are clearly a by-product of Dera Ballan's movement for change and autonomy in the religious sphere. Many of these albums and videos are financially backed by Ravidassia groups and organizations, both locally and abroad.

The demand for these videos and songs is very high among the diaspora, who have been active in uploading them on YouTube and other social media sites to counter Jatt pop music videos—sometimes resulting in an ugly war of words between the followers of both camps. There have been numerous attacks on mission singers, especially women, who often become soft targets for radical elements. While male singers receive threatening calls, women have faced physical attacks. For example, Rajni Thakarwal of Hoshiarpur was assaulted by a group of Jatt boys in

Phagwara, who demanded that she stop singing Chamara songs.[1]

Interestingly, to prevent such attacks, several militant groups, such as the Begumpura Tiger Force Punjab, Ambedkar Sena Punjab and Sri Guru Ravidas Force Punjab, have emerged to protect these singers. The groups are mostly composed of young men armed with kirpans and local weapons, who surround the stage during mission singers' performances.

Mission singers are expressing the deep-seated angst resulting from the historic mistreatment of Dalits, despite being, at least theoretically, part of the egalitarian ethos of Sikhism. The martyrdom of Sant Ramanand in Vienna, Amritbani, Seer Govardhanpur in Varanasi, Ambedkar, Begumpura and Ravidassia teachings are dominant themes in the songs of mission singers. These themes reflect the churn sparked by recent events and explain the high demand for their music, both locally and abroad. Many of these singers are invited by community members settled overseas.

The dera's popularity and influence grew multifold in the era of globalization, as the overseas population became increasingly interested in their roots. This shift changed the musical landscape of Punjab, giving Dalit singers a global platform and new opportunities.

In recent years, the substantial participation of NRIs in dera-organized pilgrimages—especially the Begumpura Express to Varanasi on the occasion of Ravidas Jayanti—bears testimony to the strong global-local linkages that the dera has established over the decades.

The trend of mission singing and its rise in popularity in Punjab has one significant common thread: Babasaheb Ambedkar, whose influence runs parallel to the masculine, pompous and sometimes violent content. Videos by these singers often feature visuals of Ambedkar, Dera Ballan and Guru Ravidas interspersed throughout.

This is not without context—Dera Ballan today displays noticeably more photos, posters and stickers of Ambedkar than even its sants. The small shops outside the dera sell calendars, metal lockets and headscarves printed with Ambedkar's images. In fact, Ambedkar's pictures occupy a prominent place in many of the dera's posters, publications and promotional materials, sometimes even overshadowing the founder of the dera, Baba Pipal Das, and other sants. It seems that Ambedkar has been seamlessly incorporated into Ravidassia religious iconography.

This reflects how the dera has, over the years, become a symbol of subaltern protest and a hub for identity articulation by the lower castes in general and the Ravidassias in particular. The dera's association with Ambedkar and his philosophy marks a kind of revival of its early association with the Ad-Dharm movement led by Babu Mangoo Ram.[2]

Babu Mangoo Ram, who was the first to articulate an independent religious identity for the Dalits of the region in the late 1920s, is believed to have been in touch with its sants, especially Sant Sarwan Das, who visited Ambedkar in Delhi.

The Ad-Dharm movement gradually petered out, and many reasons are cited for this, one of which is the rise of Ambedkar in national politics in the 1930s and his pan-Indian appeal. Ad-Dharm was gradually co-opted by Congress politics of the time and effectively surrendered its political aspirations to the emerging Dalit movement under the leadership of Ambedkar. In that sense, Ambedkar has always been integral to Dera Sachkhand Ballan.

Ambedkar's current visibility, however, is largely due to the rise of political awareness among the Dalit youth of the region. Given their history of oppression and marginalization, the legacies of Ravidas and Ambedkar coalesce rather than contradict. While the legacy of Ravidas provides a sense of autonomy and solidarity to the community through its cultural and spiritual resources, Ambedkar's presence instills modern values and a more material and pragmatic orientation.

It is no surprise, then, that many calendars and booklets sold in the shops in Varanasi and Ballan portray Ambedkar as the reincarnation of Sant Ravidas. Myth and history unite to create a symphony of resistance and a powerful political narrative of an alternative discourse.

One of the slogans that young Ravidassias are very fond of is: '*Babasaheb thaudi soch te, pahda dyange thok ke, dekh le koi rok ke*' (Babasaheb Ambedkar, we will protect and defend your legacy by becoming its shield. Let's see who stops us). The generous use of the word 'Chamar', along with 'Ravidassia', in songs and albums also resonates with the mood of the community, which clearly seeks to own its past, reassemble the fragmented pieces of its history and heroes, and reclaim the vocabulary that was once considered defamatory. This shows, among other things, the rising confidence of the Dalits in their own identity and their determination to assert it publicly.

Interestingly, the tone and tenor of mission singers and their videos have gradually become less combative. The violent and retaliatory content has waned in the years since 2009. In the immediate aftermath of the Vienna incident—where Dera Ballan's Sant Ramanand was shot dead and the gaddi nashin Sant Niranjan Das survived—the videos and songs captured the mood of the time. In 2010, a new religion, Ravidassia Dharam, was announced, and in 2012 the book Amritbani, containing the banis of Guru Ravidas, was launched in Varanasi. The martyrdom of Ramanand and the resulting anger, both in Punjab and abroad, led Dera Ballan to make certain aggressive decisions, which were reflected in the music of that period.

However, as time passed and things settled down in Ballan, the tone of mission singing changed as well. The singers still sing in honour of their guru and heroes and continue to motivate and encourage their followers, but references to 'others' have reduced or disappeared altogether. The earlier theme of 'son of Chamar versus son of Jatt' has been conspicuously absent from recent videos. Most videos are now dedicated to the banis of Guru Ravidas, featuring visuals of Seer Govardhanpur in Varanasi, Dera Ballan and its sants, and of course, plenty of Babasaheb.

Dhir, of *Putt Chamara da* (2012) fame, continues to be popular, but his recent videos—*Guru Ravidass piara* (2021), *Hun vi na jagge te fer kado jagna* (2021), *Kaum di azadi* (2022) and *Shukraana tera* (2022)—focus on themes of equality and freedom from oppression. The overall tone of these videos is to praise the guru and remind followers of their rights, alongside visuals of Ambedkar and Guru Ravidas. The palpable bitterness that had existed earlier has mellowed substantially.

Ginni Mahi and the success of *Danger Chamar*

A singer who grabbed the limelight post-2009, when mission singers mushroomed, was Ginni Mahi from Jalandhar, Punjab. She achieved overnight fame with her video *Danger Chamar* in 2016, followed by another very popular number, *Fan Baba Sahib di*, in the same year. She was interviewed by the mainstream national media and was flooded with invitations for stage performances in various cities in India and abroad, mostly from Ambedkarite and Dalit political and social groups.

Born to Rakesh Chander Mahi and Paramjit Kaur Mahi in 1998 as Gurkanwal Bharti, affectionately called Ginni, in Jalandhar, Punjab, she started singing at a young age, and her early videos were largely devotional songs dedicated to the legends of Guru Ravidas and his banis.

Her albums—*Guraan Di Diwani* (2015), *Gurupurab Hai Kanshiwale Da* (2016), *Dhol Wajde Sagatan De Vehre* (2017), *Folk Fusion* (2019) and singles, *Danger Chamar* (2016), *Haq* (2016), *Fan Baba Sahib di* (2016), *1932 Haq 2* (2017) *Suit Patiala* (2017), *Salamaan* (2018), *Raj Baba Sahib da* (2018), *Mard Daler* (2019), *Bolo jai Bhim* (2020), *Tere piche* (featuring Har Saab, 2022)—have made her the most sought-after singer in the region.

Consider the words of a few songs:

Danger Chamar (2016)

Bekhauf rehnde asi, na koi fikar na faka
Satguru Ravidas ji kende hain ji sada rakha
Kurbani dene darde na, hamesha rainde hain taiyaar
Haige asle to naalo baad
Haige asle to naalo baad
Danger Chamar

We live without fear, we carry no tension
Satguru Ravidas protects us
We don't fear sacrifice and are always ready to make sacrifices
We are more than the real weapons
We are the dangerous Chamar

Success (2020)

Guru Ravidas ji ki bachiyan
Videsha beech kittiya tarakkiyan
Ghar chhad ke bidesh bich aaya si
Change bale sapne sajaya si

The children of Guru Ravidas ji
Have prospered so much in foreign lands
Leaving their homes they came here
And realized beautiful dreams

Parnaam Mera (in Hindi)

Babasaheb tujhko hai
Parnaam mera.
Babasaheb soch aapki
Amar hai aapka naam
Manavta ka upkaar kiya
Ginni Mahi puje aapko
Aap ho mahaan
Na hua tha na hona tha
Aap jo kar gaye kaam
Manavta par tune jo upkaar kiye
Poori duniya ko nikhaar diye
Ghar ghar khushaal kiye
Paap julm ka aisa apne naash kiya
Jadd se jaativaad vriksha ukhaad diya
Babasaheb tujhko hai
Parnaam mera.

Babasaheb, I salute you
Babasaheb your thoughts,
Your name is immortal.
Ginni Mahi worships you
You are great.
Never before could someone do
What you have done.

Humanity is obliged to you
You made the world bright
And every home became happy
You destroyed oppression
And uprooted the tree of casteism
Babasaheb, I salute you!

Ginni Mahi's journey is very interesting, given the turns it has taken. One can see the gradual thematic distancing from the 'Chamara' themes in her earlier repertoire. In fact, the word has largely been absent from her songs after the *Danger Chamara* album. Instead, her songs have been dedicated to Babasaheb Ambedkar.

Looking at her songs and albums, one senses a strategic shift from catering to local audiences to aiming for a broader, pan-Indian audience. There are two possible reasons for this: one is that it was a deliberate choice to enhance her singing career by choosing themes with wider appeal and resonance, rather than limiting herself to the local politics of Punjab. The other possibility is that local politics following the Vienna shooting, combined with the lukewarm response to the subsequent movement for a separate Ravidassia religion and the launch of the book Amritbani by Dera Ballan, perhaps influenced her direction.

It is clear that Ginni's songs and videos reflect the rapidly changing local dynamics, which were initially more combative and hypermasculine—almost mimicking Jatt songs—as part of the broader Jatt versus Chamar sentiment that flared up in the aftermath of Dera Ballan's push for a separate religion. However, as tempers cooled, Ginni's songs and visuals also showed signs of mellowing. Her songs increasingly championed secular themes such as equality and harmony, avoiding issues of local inter-caste rivalry. While she continued singing devotional songs in praise of Guru Ravidas, she also began experimenting with other genres.

The young Ginni Mahi who flexed her muscles and pumped her fists in the company of male bodybuilders in the song *Danger Chamara* is now a thing of the past. Her new avatar has a multi-religious feel and a more secular tone. In one interview, she expressed her desire to become a versatile singer like the legendary Lata Mangeshkar. In another, she distanced herself from her caste identity, stating that she wants to sing all kinds of songs, not just those centred on a particular caste identity.

The two themes that have remained constant in her work are Ambedkar and Guru Ravidas. Her trademark salutation is Jai Bhim, a popular greeting among Dalit groups in honour of Babasaheb Bhim Rao Ambedkar.

Ginni's choice of songs, lyrics and visuals clearly reflects the changing local dynamics in Punjab, especially in the Doaba region. Retaining Babasaheb Ambedkar as an important theme in her work has endeared her to Ambedkarite groups from all over the country, making her shows popular in states known for vibrant Dalit movements such as Maharashtra.

In 2018, she was invited by the Deutsche Welle Global Media Forum in Germany, where she sang her popular numbers *Agar Bhim ji, Babasaheb ji is duniya me aate naa*, and *Main fan Babasaheb di*, highlighting Ambedkar's contributions to women's and Dalit empowerment in India. This international platform was met with great appreciation and pride by Ginni's fans and admirers.

However, not everyone is pleased with Ginni's new image, and some have expressed disappointment. Those who admired her *Danger Chamara* avatar and expected her to emerge as a Ravidassia icon, exclusively singing songs about Ravidas and Dera Ballan, felt let down.

While Ambedkar unites them and her salutation of Jai Bhim receives broad approval, some expected this to be echoed in unison with *Jo bole so Nirbhai*, the Ravidassia salutation. Ginni, however, has charted her own independent path, singing a variety of songs and seemingly distancing herself from being typecast solely as a Ravidassia or Dalit singer.

Interestingly, the word 'Chamara' has recently disappeared not only from Ginni's songs but also from the music scene in general. Many new singers, even those performing Ravidassia songs, are exploring all genres rather than being confined to a specific category. Words like 'Ravidassia' and 'Babasaheb' have almost overshadowed Chamara identity articulation. In her 2020 song *Success*, Ginni Mahi refers to *Guru Ravidas ke bachche* (children of Guru Ravidas), and *Babasaheb ke bachche* (children of Babasaheb), but the word 'Chamar' is notably absent.

One way to interpret this is that perhaps these singers wish to avoid direct caste identity articulation, opting instead for a broader appeal that does not offend anyone. This sentiment echoes the current mood on the ground. While people are proud of their Ravidassia identity, they are not necessarily in a retaliatory or combative mode. This reflects the response of local Ravidassias to the aggressive posturing and demands for separation from older ties, including the respect for Sikh rahit maryada. Ginni Mahi maintains her association with themes related to Guru Ravidas and Babasaheb Ambedkar, but within an inclusive framework rather than as part of a separatist agenda and politics.

Posters and their politics

Like popular songs, posters, publicity materials and calendars also offer insights into the world of the deras, their followers and their myriad ideological underpinnings. For example, Dera Ballan presents Guru Ravidas without any Vaishanavite symbols, thereby distancing itself from Hinduism and aligning with the broader nirguni nirakaar tradition of Punjab. However, in Varanasi, the tone and tenor of the calendars change, and Guru Ravidas is depicted in a Vaishanavite style, with a tilak on his forehead.

Similarly, although the shops outside Dera Ballan in Jalandhar carry all kinds of posters, calendars, souvenirs and gifts, they have very few featuring Mirabai as there is limited local demand. Mirabai posters are more popular among people from Haryana, who sometime visit the deras in Punjab to buy them.

In contrast, Mirabai occupies a prominent place in the publicity materials of the dera in Uttar Pradesh and Varanasi. In fact, the front of the boundary wall of the Janam Asthan Mandir in Seer Goverdhanpur prominently displays a mural of Mirabai and Guru Ravidas, depicting a legend from their lives.

Mirabai, known for her devotion to Lord Krishna, is also believed to have been a disciple of Guru Ravidas. Since she came from a princely Rajput community, her association with Guru Ravidas is recounted with immense pride by the Ravidassia community to underline their guru's greatness and spiritual power.

Mirabai's posters are prominently displayed on the Begumpura Express pilgrimage train from Jalandhar to Varanasi. However, within the Dera Ballan premises, Mirabai posters are rare. The presence and absence of these symbols and imagery are not without cultural contexts; they reflect broader socio-cultural and historical constructs. Varanasi and Haryana, in comparison to Punjab, represent the saguni ecosystem, while Punjab is known for its nirguni traditions, which explains the prominence given to Mirabai in these pockets of Dera Ballan.

On various occasions, such as Valmiki Jayanti or Ravidas Jayanti, Jalandhar is covered with all kinds of posters. During Ravidas Jayanti, one rarely, if ever, sees a Sikh guru on posters put up by Ravidassia groups and organizations. In contrast, posters for Valmiki Jayanti include images of all prominent saints, in addition to Maharishi Valmiki, such as Ravidas, Balaknath, Guru Nanak, Kabir and sometimes even Hindu gods and goddesses. Given the strained relationship between Jatt Sikhs and Ravidassias in the region, Dera Ballan and other Ravidassia groups tend to distance themselves from Sikh symbols and icons.

These posters are so closely tied to their regional, local and religious contexts that if, for instance, one sees a van full of people arriving outside the Jalandhar station with Mirabai posters all over it to board the Begumpura Express, one can easily guess that they are from Haryana.

Headscarves sold in the shops outside Dera Ballan prominently feature Bob Marley, Che Guevara and flags of Canada and other European countries, alongside images of sants and Babasaheb Ambedkar. This is because a large number of the visitors to Dera Ballan are from Punjab, with a significant number either settled abroad or aspiring to obtain a visa. These shops are adept at sensing visitors' preferences and customizing their products accordingly.

In contrast, headscarves in Varanasi lack this variety, offering only plain saffron or white options, except during Ravidas Jayanti, when a large contingent of followers from abroad arrives to celebrate the birth anniversary of their guru, prompting some shops to offer a more colourful range of products. Likewise, the syncretic accommodation of symbols from neighbouring religions and faiths is common in Valmiki temples and posters but not so much in Ravidassia representations. This should be understood and contextualized within the broader socio-cultural and regional history of the Valmiki community.

The point is that these posters convey much more than they show and are imbued with a range of emotions and meanings. They reflect the overall mood of local or regional politics and its changing contours. More subtly, they also signify closeness or distance from one group or another. For instance, around 2010, the Begumpura Express bogies featured more posters of Maharishi Valmiki. In the early days following the Vienna incident, Dera Ballan forefronted the spirit of larger Dalit mobilization while promoting the Ravidassia identity, assuming it would be enthusiastically accepted by other groups. However, this was not the case, as groups such as the Valmikis expressed their annoyance and distanced themselves from Dera Ballan's efforts to establish a separate religious identity.

The same goes for the music of the region. The gradual disappearance of the Chamara theme from the songs of Ginni Mahi and other singers from the region reflects the changing cultural and political undercurrents. At the very least, it signifies a thaw in the antagonism and belligerence that had emerged in the immediate aftermath of the Vienna incident.

Trends in imagery and music particularly reflect the undercurrents of a society and its turmoil. They echo the subterranean, subconscious core of the collective psyche and reveal messages that are often muted in the everyday world. Calendar art, for instance, can be a powerful record of anguish, aspirations and regional politics. Likewise, music provides a medium to express the angst of the voiceless. Both can be markers of protest and a countercurrent to an unequal world.

8

The Myriad Hues of Deras in Punjab

If there is one thing that symbolizes the culture of deras in Punjab and the northwest, it is the mind-boggling diversity displayed in the region. Besides those already discussed, the area has numerous other deras that capture the limelight every now and then. They contribute to the fluidity of the concept, resisting any attempt to fit it into a conceptual box.

One of the oldest deras in the region, Radha Soami Satsang Beas (RSSB) is almost a township, planned and constructed on a vast stretch of land along the banks of the river Beas in Amritsar, Punjab. Its founder, Jaimal Singh, who was initiated by Shiv Dayal Singh of Agra (the founder of the Radha Soami Satsang tradition) settled in an isolated spot outside the town of Beas after he retired from the British Indian army. There, he began spreading the teachings of his guru, Shiv Dayal Singh (1818–1878).

The settlement soon grew into a colony and became known as Dera Baba Jaimal Singh, which is now the world centre of the Radha Soami Satsang Beas. Shiv Dayal Singh's philosophy, like many traditions in the region at the time, borrowed from the popular syncretic traditions that were deeply influenced by the esoteric mysticism prevalent in north India during eighteenth and nineteenth centuries. His parents were followers of Guru Nanak and Sant Tulsi Saheb of Hathras, who preached *santmat* (the collective wisdom of a group of sants) and the unity of philosophical thoughts.

Dera Beas emerged within this philosophical context, which emphasized the role of a mentor who promoted the coexistence of traditions and highlighted the value of the inner spiritual journey.

Even though the centre was in Agra, the founder was from Punjab. With the emergence of Agra as an important cantonment town during the British Raj, many people from Punjab moved there in search of opportunities. Later, when Dera Beas was established and flourished in Punjab, it retained its syncretic ethos.

An interesting feature of all five sants of the Radha Soami Satsang Beas to date is that they were all from the upper/dominant caste of Khatri/Jatt lineage. Additionally, they were all educated, with some even having backgrounds in fields such as engineering and law. In fact, Jassdeep Singh Gill, the newly appointed (2 September 2024) spiritual head of the Dera has a doctorate in chemical engineering from Cambridge university.

The dera does not promote any overt caste identity and claims to be open to the rich and poor alike. However, it is often perceived as catering to the urban, rich middle-class population, who visit the dera as a spiritual retreat away from the din and bustle of everyday life.

Many of the functionaries working at the Beas secretariat are retired bureaucrats and police officers. From the entry gate to the reception, offices, langar halls and satsang areas, the set-up evokes a high-end corporate ambience rather than the typically unstructured, even chaotic, atmosphere of religious spaces brimming with devotees.

Unlike Dera Ballan, for example, RSSB appears to be apolitical. It is believed that the founder of Dera Sacha Sauda, Beparwah Mastana Baluchistani, was also initiated at Dera Beas under the mentorship of Sant Sawan Singh, the second sant of the dera. Beparwah Mastana later founded his own centre in Sirsa.

'Freezer Baba' at Nurmahal Dera

Barely an hour's drive from Dera Beas lies another dera that has been in the news for the mysterious samadhi of its guru, Ashutosh Maharaj. The dera is popularly known as Divya Jyoti Jagran Sansthan (DJJS) or simply Dera Nurmahal.

Born as Mahesh Jha in the Darbhanga district of Bihar in 1946, his journey to becoming a dera chief in Punjab—with dozens of centres in the country and abroad and its headquarters at Pitampura, Delhi—has all the ingredients of a potboiler. It involves suspense, drama, big property disputes and most notably, a baba whose body has been preserved by his followers in a -22 degree Celsius freezer since he was declared clinically dead in 2014. Followers believe that the baba is in samadhi, a spiritual state of meditation, and that he will return to life after some years.

Located on a sprawling campus, Dera Nurmahal was established by Ashutosh Maharaj in 1983. One narrative suggests that after leaving his wife and son in Bihar, Ashutosh lived the life of a wanderer in Delhi and Punjab. He was initiated into the Manav Utthan Seva Samiti of Satpal Maharaj in Uttarakhand before eventually settling down in Nurmahal, Punjab. Initially, he organized religious satsangs in nearby villages and towns before establishing DJJS on the Jalandhar-Nakodar road. He had it registered in 1991, with New Delhi as its headquarters.

Like other Deras, DJJS claims lakhs of followers from all religions and castes, spread across the country and globally. The dera previously courted controversy with Sikh organizations, who accused the DJJS and its guru of diluting the messages of the Sikh bani and misrepresenting the philosophy of the gurus.

On 19 January 2014, however, things changed with the 'death' of Ashutosh Maharaj, who was initially declared clinically dead by doctors. Messages were sent to politicians and followers announcing his passing. However, the situation and narrative changed quickly with the arrival of functionaries from the Delhi-based headquarters. The dera then decided to preserve the body of the guru in a deep freezer, claiming that he was in deep meditation and would awaken from his spiritual slumber after several years. Many believe this was part of a strategy to prevent the organization from becoming mired in a succession controversy and to keep the multi-million dollar empire intact.

On 1 December 2014, the Punjab and Haryana High Court ordered that the last rites of Ashutosh Maharaj be performed within fifteen days. The ruling, however, was later suspended.[1] After many twists and turns, in July 2017, the Punjab and Haryana High Court granted the followers permission to continue preserving his body in a freezer.[2]

A government-designated team of doctors and experts periodically visits the dera to check the status of the body, ensuring it is being preserved properly and monitoring for signs of decay. Meanwhile, the activities of the dera have continued as before, including satsangs and annual Guru Purnima congregations.

The dera is also known for its work in providing education to the blind, poor children and even jail inmates, including those at the Tihar Jail in Delhi. In addition, the dera runs a cattle semen bank with around 125 high-quality bulls, and their *gaushala* (cowshed) houses more than 900 Indian-breed cows.

By some accounts, the popularity of the dera has dwindled after the passing of the guru, with fewer politicians visiting. However, according to one dera source, the organization has some sixty-five branches in Punjab alone and is active in nearly twenty countries. Clearly, the dera remains relevant.

Nonetheless, controversies continue to dog it, as succession claims and counterclaims continue to surface. A man named Dilip Kumar Jha from Bihar, claiming to be the son of Ashutosh Maharaj, has sought the court's intervention to have his father's body handed over to him for the death rituals in Bihar.

The DJJS largely follows Hindu religious traditions but, like other deras, it also experiments and blends its teachings with elements from other traditions to appeal to and align with local sensibilities. Moreover, there is a sense of equality that most of these deras consciously maintain within their premises, given the prevalent social inequalities and caste distinctions.

Dera Bhaniarawale

In Ropar district, nestled deep in a forest, lies Dera Piara Singh Bhaniarawale in the village of Dhamiana. The dera became controversial when its guru, Piara Singh, was attacked by radical forces for propagating an alternative spiritual path and introducing a holy book called *Bhavsagar Granth*.

Piara Singh was a Class IV government employee with the horticulture department. His father used to look after two mazaars on the outskirts of Dhamiana. After his father's death, Piara Singh took over the upkeep of the mazaars and, over time, started preaching and attending to general health ailments and other problems of those who came to the shrine seeking his healing touch.

Piara Singh was from the Mazhabi Sikh/Valmiki community. As his influence gradually spread in the surrounding areas and his followers increased, politicians of various affiliations also started visiting him. One of his prominent followers was Buta Singh, who served as home minster from 1986 to 1989. He used to visit the dera with his wife to seek Piara Singh's blessings, as she suffered from various health-related issues.

Over time, Piare Singh's popularity grew significantly, leading to frequent conflicts with fundamentalist forces who believed his approach to religiosity was contrary to Sikh maryada. Although the dera claimed to be open to all, it was largely seen as a Valmiki Samaj establishment. The relationship between fundamentalist Sikh groups and Dera Bhaniara remained fraught with conflict.

In one instance, it is believed that a follower of Bhaniara Baba was denied permission to carry the Guru Granth Sahib from the local gurudwara for a religious function at his home. This led to a demand by the followers of the dera to have their own granth. This incident became a catalyst for the compilation of a separate granth of 2704 pages, called Bhavsagar Samundar Amrit Vani, which was released by the baba on Baisakhi in 2001. Baba Bhaniara's followers began holding religious ceremonies with the Bhavsagar Granth as the central focus. Sikh organizations took offence to this, and Baba Bhaniara was accused of sacrilege.

In September 2001, members of a newly formed group called Khalsa Action Force attacked a function in Ludhiana where the Bhavsagar Granth was being used by dera followers. It was said that the Bhavsagar Granth had copied many portions of the Guru Granth Sahib, and that a few pictures of Bhaniara Baba resembled the tenth guru of the Sikhs—both of which were considered blasphemous by the Sikhs. This led to a cycle of violence and counter-violence between the followers of Dera Bhaniara and the Sikhs.

Bhaniarawale was excommunicated by the Akal Takht, and his followers were asked to apologize. Copies of the Bhavsagar Granth were confiscated and destroyed by government agencies. There were attempts by radical forces to physically harm Piara Singh, and many court cases were filed against him, but he survived them all.

He eventually died of cardiac arrest in 2019. His sprawling dera, spread over 100 acres in Dhamiana and built with the help of his followers, continues to attract thousands on the 26th day of every month, when a *bhandara* is organized and his son, Satnam Singh, presides over the congregation.

Satnam Singh Bhaniarawale

In the winter of 2022, a trip to Dera Bhaniarawale led to a late-evening meeting with Satnam Singh, the current chief. The dera's gigantic gate is decorated with statues of various animals, including a horse and peacocks. At the top of the gate, concrete sculptures of cows and calves are prominently displayed. Two ferocious-looking lions on either side of the gate add to the mystery, as do the subsequent rings of police barricades.

After a thorough security check, the staff made a call to the dera chief to discuss my credentials, then asked a few questions regarding the reason for my visit before granting me entry.

Satnam Singh lives in the dera campus with his wife and children and leads an overtly domestic life. During our meeting, he came across as an unassuming character, without the usual frills and aura associated with a baba.

The walls of his room were covered with photo calendars representing every possible tradition of the region, including Guru Govind Singh, Baba Khijra, Goddess Lakshmi and of course, Ravidas and Valmiki. There was nothing to suggest that any one tradition held primacy over the others. Although the dera and its sants belong to the Valmiki community, there was no particular emphasis on that caste identity in the way the room was arranged and decorated. It was clear that the dera was consciously trying to move away from any singular identity or conflict with anyone. The pictures on the wall testified to the dera's deliberate syncretic positioning after its early turbulent years, when it appeared to challenge Sikhism through a new holy book and alternative positioning.

Although Satnam Singh appeared easygoing and unassuming, his views were often revolutionary. He quoted Ambedkar as the messiah of the downtrodden who advocated for education, but asked, 'What about those who could not study?' He then answered his own query, 'They should take up arms, lathis, to defend their right to a dignified life. They must not do manual labour for daily wages unnecessarily.' His anger seemed directed against all dominating forces, as he defined 'Dalit' as those who were poor and economically marginalized, irrespective of caste.

To highlight unity and togetherness, the dera adopted a trishul—a prominently Hindu religious symbol—with an extra prong to represent unity among four major religious traditions: Hindu, Muslim, Christian and Sikh.

Satnam Singh is critical of Dalit leadership, accusing them of not being committed to uplifting their society and instead focusing on self-promotion and aggrandizement. He cited the case of Dera Ballan, which he believes is promoting and fostering one particular caste identity, thereby undermining the potential for a broader lower-caste coalition in the region.

Satnam Singh advocates the idea of two langars: one for human beings and another for animals and birds. The dera looks after stray animals in the adjoining forested area. The organization has also invested in maintaining ponds and forest areas by initiating tree plantation drives on special occasions.

Unlike other deras, there is not much gloss or glitz here. However, the large acreage of land occupied by the dera, along with its influence on the surrounding areas and its experiments in religious philosophy that challenge the mainstream, make it a prominent dera.

This is despite the fact that, following the passing of Piara Singh—and even before that in recent years—the dera has been rather subdued and out of the limelight. The monthly congregation or samagam of devotees, however, continues to be a well-attended event. The dera's influence in the surrounding areas keeps it politically significant, especially as it is perceived as representing the Valmiki Samaj, an important and decisive segment of the electoral landscape in the region.

Satnam Singh led me to the gate of his residence, inviting me to visit again. Beyond his ideas, what stayed with me were his characteristic chuckles, interspersed throughout his long monologues, which he used to convey his exasperation with anything he did not like.

As I took my leave with folded hands and asked for directions to Khuralgarh, his trademark chuckle returned as he uttered the name of Satwinder Heera.

Khuralgarh and Charan Chhoh Ganga

If Dera Sachkhand Ballan has emerged as one of the major centres of Ravidassia identity articulation, it also has many counterpoints. One of these is the group that projects Khuralgarh as the central site of Guru Ravidas's historical legacy and legends. This group aligns itself with the Ad-Dharmi model, prominently displays the symbol 'Soham' and demonstrates its dedication to the ideology of Babu Mangoo Ram and Banta Ram Gheda—who is credited with identifying the birthplace of Guru Ravidas in Seer Govardhanpur, which is now under the complete control of Dera Ballan.

Kharali or Khuralgarh is in Garhshankar in Hoshiarpur district, in a hilly, forested location on the border between Punjab and Himachal Pradesh. It is believed that Guru Ravidas visited this place and spent some time here preaching about social equality and a non-hierarchical world view where everyone is equal in the eyes of god.

According to legend, Guru Ravidas's popularity among the people of the area soon soared, making the local king, Bain Singh, insecure. Some upper-caste individuals complained to the king that Guru Ravidas was instigating people against the Hindu religion. This infuriated the king, and he ordered the guru's imprisonment, sentencing him to work on a grain grinder called *kharas*. Guru Ravidas initially pleaded with the king, attempting to explain that he was not preaching against any religion but rather advocating a philosophy of equality. But the king remained unrelenting and insisted on punishing the guru.

Once in prison, Guru Ravidas meditated, and the kharas began working on its own. When news of this miracle reached the king, he came running to the guru with his family to ask for mercy and forgiveness. As the legend goes, Guru Ravidas not only forgave him but also responded generously to the king's request to make the area water-rich, as the region was suffering from water scarcity.

Guru Ravidas walked three miles down a hill and touched a stone with his toe. The moment he did this, the Ganga burst forth from a small aperture. The guru instructed the king to keep walking, assuring him that the water would follow. However, at some distance, the king grew suspicious and looked back to see if the stream of water was following him. The moment he looked back, the water disappeared.

Charan Chhoh Ganga is believed to be the spot where the miracle occurred, and today, a temple stands there to commemorate the legend. This place is now managed by the All India Adi-Dharam Mission, under the care of a group led by Sant Satwinder Singh Heera. It is located about three miles from the main Khuralgarh Sahib, aligning with the legend. Two different groups now manage these sites, and there is a palpable sense of rivalry between them.

Satwinder Singh Heera comes across as an articulate, well-travelled person who, along with his family, has been actively engaged in developing this site as a sacred space where Guru Ravidas lived and preached. Sant Heera's personal journey is no less adventurous or legendary.

Hailing from Ludhiana, Sant Heera, by his own admission, initially worked in Libya as an engineer, closely associated with Colonel Gaddafi's team. His children are now well settled, many of them abroad. His son is a pilot, and his daughter-in-law's father is now his associate, serving as the chairman of Shri Charan Chhoh Ganga at Sachkhand Shri Khural Garh Sahib.

Well versed in communication, finance and management, Sant Satwinder Heera travels extensively to build new networks across the country, guided by the legends surrounding Guru Ravidas. Like Banta Ram Gheda, Satwinder Heera has a penchant for identifying legendary spots from the life of Guru Ravidas. He has visited states like Madhya Pradesh, Gujarat, Telangana, Bihar, Uttarakhand and Rajasthan in search of places associated with the legends of Guru Ravidas. His enthusiasm for his work is evident when he claims, 'It appears that Guru Ravidas had even visited the Pope.'

Satwinder Singh Heera is well known among the Ravidassia groups from Ballan in Jalandhar and Seer Govardhanpur in Varanasi. However, he himself 'hates' the term 'Ravidassia' and finds it 'inappropriate'.

Given that Ballan Dera currently holds a prominent position in articulating the political aspirations of the community and has been aggressively pursuing much of Guru Ravidas' legacy, other groups—such as Satwinder Heera's—that continue to follow the Ad-Dharm framework, which differs significantly from Dera Ballan's world view, feel sidelined. The bitterness surrounding the term 'Ravidassia' stems from this background.

It is no surprise that in Satwinder Heera's calendars and posters, there is a special request to the sangat to identify themselves as Ad-Dharmi during the census. Notably, Dera Ballan has been advocating for 'Ravidassia' as a new religious identity instead of 'Ad-Dharmi'.

Whether it is Baba Jaure of Ballan or Sant Satwinder Heera, they all tend to unite in opposition to Dera Sachkhand Ballan. Heera, in fact, feels the term 'dera' does not do justice to the philosophy of Guru Ravidas. According to him, the concept of a dera accords primacy to the idea of a human guru, which he believes is irreverent to the ultimate guru, Guru Ravidas. Consequently, he dislikes the term 'dera' and instead refers to his place as a Guru Ravidas temple, which is decorated with the Ad-Dharmi 'Soham' symbol.

Other buildings constructed around the temple are dedicated to Banta Ram Gheda and Babu Mangoo Ram, the stalwart and founder of the Ad-Dharm movement. One building is named the Babu Mangoo Ram Mugowal Yaadgaari Hall (Babu Mangoo Ram Mugowal Memorial Hall), while the adjoining one is named after Banta Ram Gheda as the Baba Banta Ram Gheda Yaadgari Sahit Sangeet Academy.

The temple premises include a kharas, believed to be one of those used by Guru Ravidas while in prison, safely kept in a transparent glass case. The spots where the first stream of water erupted and where it subsequently stopped are considered sacred, and both locations feature statues of Guru Ravidas.

At one of these spots, devotees offer toy aeroplanes and baby boy dolls, a sight typical of the area. The aeroplanes signify aspirations for overseas migration, while the baby boy dolls perhaps represent the hopes of childless couples wishing for a son. Punjab has traditionally been known for its culture of son preference, which has contributed to the skewed female-male sex ratio in the region.

The organization runs langars and supports the education of orphaned children from the surrounding areas. Sant Satwinder Singh Heera's visitors' room was covered with posters of Dalit icons like Ambedkar, Mangoo Ram and others, as well as numerous pictures of both Valmiki and Ravidas. This is intended to drive home the point that focusing on a singular caste is politically counter-productive. The establishment such as this one essentially are counters to the Dera Ballan and its movement. The differences and disagreements are quite prevalent and ongoing.

An overnight stay in the organization's guest room shed light on everyday life at Charan Chhoh Ganga. There were young boys, introduced as orphans, who were serving tea and helping with daily chores, along with some older folks like Buddhu Das from Sagar district, Madhya Pradesh.

Buddhu Das was there to construct a rest house for himself and others. He had donated Rs 1 lakh and wished to spend the rest of his life at the dera. His family was aware of his decision, but he was committed to the cause of his community and did not wish to return. He shared that he had also built a temple dedicated to Guru Ravidas in his hometown.

Another person actively involved in managing all the arrangements was Inderdev Kesari, a graduate from Ghajipur, Uttar Pradesh, who had come to contribute to the efforts of Sant ji.

Early in the morning, as the place reverberated with Ravidas bhajans and the chirping of birds, Satwinder Jeet Singh Heera met us over tea. As always, he carried a silver nishaan sahib or insignia of the Ad-Dharm in his hand. The children came one by one to touch his feet before boarding a cab to a nearby school.

Buddhu Ram's selflessness, Inderdev's renunciatory spirit and Satwinder Heera's journey from Ludhiana to Libya and then to Charan Chhoh together create a collage of emotions that haunt, unsettle and provoke reflection at the same time.

Sant Heera's largely family-run enterprise seems poised to take off towards broader and larger aspirations. However, as one leaves the place, the most lasting image is that of the lonely septuagenarian Buddhu Ram and the young boys who served tea, both lingering in the shadow of a larger meta-narrative called Satwinder Jeet Heera.

All these establishments are deras. The media often broadbrushes them all in a single colour. To the outside world, they are largely seen as either a blind spot or a deviant narrative involving some baba or sant, often found on the wrong side of the law. It is evident that the vast spectrum of deras and their cultures signifies a heady mix of the esoteric and the everyday, politics and power games, the sacred and the sinful—all in varying degrees, with the presence or absence of certain features creating a unique identity for each one.

Despite some overlaps, each of these deras has a specific, locally embedded genealogy and therefore deserves to be studied and understood not as part of a larger universe but as a distinct microcosm.

Epilogue

India's—perhaps even South Asia's—religious landscape does not have many straight lines. And straight lines are good for making neat and tidy silos. Much of Indian society's current churning over its sacred geography is due to the enmeshment of its multitude of faiths and their entangled moorings. Fundamentalists of all hues like silos and dislike this organic uniqueness that defies tidy cartography and architecture.

Porousness and permeability are two distinct features of Indian religions. Centuries of coexistence have created an eternal continuum that cuts across cultures and faiths. People and groups crossed over, yet they retained their linkages through rituals, folk traditions, symbols and motifs.

It is this ability to carry many pasts into the present that make Indian civilization so distinctive. Faiths are fluid and carry a natural propensity to engage in dialogue. It was the colonial cartographic exercises—like the census—that first introduced a sense of separateness among the communities and imposed an identity rubric that demarcated boundaries. Thus began a churning that involved great stress and an interrogation of the naturalness of community existence, of give and take and mutuality.

The deras and their cultural setting represent a microcosm of that churning in the realm of religion in contemporary times. Deras, as we understand, have multiple narratives around their emergence and expansion. They can be understood through many frameworks. However, the most compelling framework is the idea that deras are essentially seats of philosophical argumentation and debate.

At the core of the phenomenon of the emergence and mushrooming of deras lies a difference in world views, leading to the creation of new spaces. Along with caste, this tradition of argumentation constitutes the essence of dera culture. Deras are emblematic of regional socio-political and economic conditions and their stresses. At the same time, they reflect philosophical churning.

In the case of Dera Ballan, for instance, its genealogy is marked by splits and counterarguments with the mainstream. Dera Ballan voiced its differences with the Sikh tradition in its quest for an equal space. Yet the possibility of further internal churning remains, as it has many detractors who question its politics and constitution from within the caste framework.

Each dera carries its own unique philosophy and raison d'etre. In the South Asian context, subaltern castes have found it difficult to integrate with the mainstream, as the locality of caste challenged their aspirations for equality and inclusion. As a result, whenever these communities achieved stability and success—especially in economic terms—they rebelled. In most cases, the rebellion reflected alterations within the paradigm of continuity and change.

It is therefore important to understand these deras in terms of their cultural grounding and their regional and caste histories. Interestingly, there is no etymological indication of any caste orientation within these deras. They are as benign as a temple, gurudwara, ashram or shrine could be. Yet, in practice, due to multiple socio-cultural reasons, deras have come to be recognized as sites for subalterns and the underclass.

Even deras like Dera Sacha Sauda, which has no particular caste orientation, have a significant base among the Dalits of the region. Mainstream religious traditions have favoured the upper strata and their hegemonic presence, largely due to their economic and cultural capital. Sikhism, for instance, branched off from Hinduism and eventually emerged as a mainstream religion in its own right. In fact, it began with a strong philosophical foundation rooted in equality and justice. Theoretically, it remains undiluted on that front.

Yet in practice, caste-like formations gradually emerged, and the Jatts—a land-owning community—came to occupy the dominant caste status, and increasingly monopolized religio-cultural spaces. This dominance was replicated across villages and towns through stories of discrimination in public spaces against individuals from lower-caste backgrounds.

As a result, deras began to proliferate, forming around various axes. Some clustered around Ravidas, others around Kabir and some around Valmiki, among others. Even within these deras, differences emerged in terms of rahit maryada and the degree of engagement with the past. For instance, Dera Ballan continues to incorporate traditions and rituals drawn from multiple sources, such as Udasis, Sikhism and others.

A broad view of the religious landscape of India's northwest, in particular, reveals that while silos were constructed through the census and other such tools during the nineteenth and twentieth centuries, many people from the bottom of the caste hierarchy remained free-floating and in search of equal treatment.

In the run-up to independence, caste-based collective articulations—many of them reformist—gained momentum. Babu Mangoo Ram's journey is a prime example of this trend: from being a Ghadarite in California to working among his caste brethren in Hoshiarpur, Punjab, with schools run by the Arya Samaj, and eventually laying the foundation of Ad-Dharm, which was then recognized as a separate religious group by the 1931 Census.

Post-independence, Dr B.R. Ambedkar's efforts to voice the concerns of the oppressed and the marginalized gave momentum to and strengthened the politics of collectivization among the lower castes. Ambedkar led by example, advocating a counter-philosophy within the realm of religion as he critiqued the caste system prevalent in India and eventually embraced Buddhism in protest.

Many of the deras of Punjab, such as Dera Sachkhand of Ballan, have retained that streak of political activism and counter-current culture. It is no wonder, then, that they have embraced Ambedkar as part of their sanctum sanctorum, making him an integral part of their religious iconography. This integration of Ambedkar is reflected in the prominent display of his photos, cut-outs and billboards in and around dera premises in Jalandhar and other places. In fact, many deras have dedicated sections in their libraries to Ambedkar's writings, books and commentaries.

Another interesting feature of these deras is their aspirational quest for equality. This sentiment overrides the fissiparous tendencies prevalent in these times. For example, Sant Baba Phool Nath Dera, near Jalandhar, has huge portraits of Ambedkar in its premises.

The dera reflects not only ordinary existential anxieties and aspirations—such as dreams of an overseas job, which are typical of the region and symbolized in the offerings of toy planes in the sanctum sanctorum—but also the urge for a larger, interwoven collective shaped by composite narratives drawn from Ambedkar's life stories and the legends of Guru Ravidas and other saints.

One of the paintings at Sant Baba Phool Nath Dera sums up the prevailing mood. The painting depicts Ravidas, Valmiki and Kabir walking alongside the Buddha, followed by Ambedkar and his band of followers. Visuals such as this underscore the inner churning and give expression to the collective urge of the subaltern castes and communities for a grand alliance, subsuming all fissiparous narratives and ideologies.

Imagining a big banyan tree

Is there anything pathological about the mushrooming of these deras? The answer is likely 'yes' for fundamentalists, but 'no' for those who view their emergence as organic to the very idea of religion in India, which has argumentative philosophy at its core. The more one travels, the more one realizes that there is no finality to the world of ideas. Ideas, especially in the realm of the sacred, are inherently hybrid and have an inbuilt propensity for cross-fertilization. Branching off becomes everyday and ordinary.

The South Asian imagination of the religious landscape resembles a gigantic and ancient banyan tree, where it is difficult to distinguish between the main trunk and its offshoots that, over time, have come into their own and developed an independent vertical identity. Over time, the tree becomes so huge and dense that its multitude of branches creates a microcosmic forest. A wanderer would likely either get lost or confused in search of the original trunk. Such is the entanglement and enmeshment of faiths in the subcontinent. The deras, too, are part of a similar universe. They number in the thousands in Punjab, and they continue to grow.

This is, however, a progressive view of the deras. Indeed, many are run by individuals as personal enterprises. Such deras are plentiful, and they have prospered for various reasons. Many continue to grab the limelight for unscrupulous reasons and the misadventures of their leaders. Even these deras attract a large share of the free-floating underclass of followers from the region and beyond.

However, these deras have no political pivot—no Ambedkar, no Phule and not even a pretence of such awareness. They operate as purely entrepreneurial ventures, investing in brand-building through films, charity work like blood donation camps and mass marriages for poor couples and hobnobbing with the powers that be. Politicians of all stripes are understandably therefore ever willing to warm up as they are also sites of vote banks. It is no surprise that the political patronage these deras receive in times of crisis exposes their underground connections.

Old deras prosper. New ones emerge. Congregations grow larger. A dera in Punjab continues to preserve the body of its main guru in a freezer in anticipation of his return from samadhi. Another dera in Haryana and its followers await the return of its sant, who is in jail, believing him to have been unfairly framed by the drug mafia. The dera, which is practically a township, has its own schools, colleges, restaurants, hospitals and a sports complex. There is a dense network of CCTV cameras, with loudspeakers placed in every nook and cranny. Wherever one goes, the speakers continuously relay the jailed sant's recorded discourses on the morally correct way of living.

This island-like dera has an obsession with miniaturizing anything and everything. Many of its buildings and structures mimic European architectural styles, making it evident that the dera leader fancies creating a kingdom-like space for his abode. The main place of worship, commemorating Sant Satnam, retains its old charm and simplicity, yet everything else has a celluloid feel.

As one looks out at the township in amazement from the top of one of its spectacular hotels with a rooftop swimming pool, it becomes clear that these deras play on ordinary people's insecurities and their urge to be close to a make-believe world—a dream space that distances them from the harsh realities of everyday struggles.

The dera has a substantial presence of followers from nearby villages and towns in Haryana and Rajasthan, as well as a sizeable number of families from Bihar, Madhya Pradesh and Uttar Pradesh working in various capacities, mainly in manual jobs like sweeping, gardening and cleaning. Most of them, invariably with stories of deprivation and family struggles, have ended up here to find refuge in this make-believe world.

In the leader's absence, the enterprise is being well looked after by his adopted daughter, Ruhani Didi. The dera remains as alive and active as ever, even as the baba tries for yet another furlough.

Elsewhere, while Dera Ballan remains relatively quiet, Surinder Baba of Kahnpur is preparing for yet another overseas sojourn. Clearly, the world is big enough to accommodate both: the sublime and the base, the sacred and the profane, the bizarre and the ordinary. The world of deras and their followers has ample space for them to exist and prosper in all their varied forms. The point is, one must be careful not to club them all together under one rubric, as doing so would impoverish our world of knowledge.

Finally, a little story from Patiala

This book began with an anecdote, and so it must end with one too. My research project on the agribusiness farms of Patiala ended abruptly after I moved to Delhi. However, not everything ended with the project. A few years later, I happened to be in Patiala for an academic assignment. I was told that my research assistant from my old project, a bright and hardworking Sikh girl had enrolled there as a research student. I was curious to meet her, and my hosts arranged a meeting.

We met in the late afternoon. It was Shivratri that day, an auspicious day for Hindus and an important festival. We chatted about our respondents and fondly remembered the village where we had conducted our fieldwork. She was married now, as was obvious from her elbow-length *chudaa*—the traditional bangles worn by Punjabi women that signify marital status. As we finished our tea, she grew anxious to leave as it was getting late. She was in a hurry, she confided, as her husband was waiting downstairs—they were going to a Shiva temple to offer milk at the *shivling*.

As she left, I was filled with a sense of awe at the illuminating syncretism present in our everyday world. It is in these moments that the idea of India and its religious landscape truly shine. The world of deras, with its immense complexity and multilayeredness, is like a dense, deep forest that invites knowledge-seekers to undertake a journey full of serendipitous moments and encounters, defying any standard obsession with monoliths.

Acknowledgements

All journeys have milestones, both in terms of people and places. Throughout my decade-long wandering for research on deras in Punjab, Haryana and Varanasi, I had the good fortune of being supported, encouraged and assisted by many friends, co-travellers and critics. I extend my heartfelt gratitude to all of them. A small research grant early on and a generous environment for conducting research by Dr B.R. Ambedkar University Delhi helped a great deal in pursuing this research. Moreover, the university's excellent interdisciplinary pedagogical framework that brought the best minds together indeed enriched my perspectives and research orientations.

As I travelled, I also wrote as and when I felt like it—not when the norms of career progression demanded it. This obviously had a price, but it was insignificant compared to the joy of being free from the dictates of academic red tape. Meaningful writing should flow from the heart like poetry and attempt to engage with the people at large. Many of my writings were published in both academic journals and the popular press, and many appeared as chapters in edited volumes.

I wish to particularly acknowledge the *Economic and Political Weekly* for publishing my early dera work as articles. I would also like to thank Brill Publishers, Primus Books, Rawat

Publications and their erudite editors for their interest in my work and for giving them space in various book projects. A few chapters in this book are adapted versions of some of these, which have been reworked and updated to fit into the flow of this monograph.

Thanks to Papa, Mummy and Mummy-in-law for their encouragement and support; to my wife Anjali, and sons, Ayushmaan and Shriman, for consistently reminding me about what seemed to be a never-ending book project when they saw me absent from my study table for weeks altogether; to brothers Rajesh and Ashutosh, sisters-in-law Sonali and Asha, nieces Suhani and Anya, and nephews Aaryaman and Anshuman for being there in the journey called life with their best wishes. To Niraj–Mrigya and their kids Arihaan and Aarna—love you all and thanks.

Last but not least, had it not been for a very patient and scholarly Karthik Venkatesh, my commissioning editor, and his *Punjabi by dil se* status, this book would have simply not happened. I owe it to you, Karthik, for your trust in me and the idea of the book. Thank you so much. Cheers.

Notes

Foreword: The Power of Deras

1 Translation by John Stratton Hawley and the author in John Stratton Hawley and Mark Juergensmeyer, *Songs of the Saints of India*, New York: Oxford University Press, 1988, p. 9.

2 Mark Juergensmeyer, *Religion as Social Vision: The Movement against Untouchability in 20th Century Punjab*, Berkeley: University of California Press, 1982. It has been reprinted in India under the title *Religious Rebels in the Punjab: The Ad Dharm Challenge to Caste*, New Delhi: Navayana Publishing, 2004.

3 Ibid., p. 84.

4 Clifford Geertz, 'Centres, Kings, and Charisma: Reflections on the Symbolics of Power', in *Culture and its Creators: Essays in Honour of Edward Shils*, eds. Joseph Ben-David and Terry Nichols Clark, Chicago: University of Chicago Press, 1977, p. 151.

5 D.L. Kapur, *Heaven on Earth*, Beas: Radhasoami Satsang, p. 28.

6 See the Radha Soami family tree by David C. Lane in Mark Juergensmeyer, *Radhasoami Reality: The Logic of a Modern Faith*, Princeton: Princeton University Press, 1991. A revised and updated version of the book, with a vastly larger family tree, is slated to be published in 2025 by Oxford University Press.

Preface

1 Source: Not known. Ram Swaroop remembered the song as sung by his people in daily gatherings. Translation by the author.

2 Santosh K. Singh, 'Dalit Politics and its fragments in Punjab: Does religion hold the key?', *Economic and Political Weekly* Vol LIII no. 35, 1, September 2018, pp. 32–36. A chapter in this volume includes a developed and updated version of this piece and other EPW articles on dera by the author.

Chapter 1: The Story of a Village in Punjab: Mapping the Sacred Geography

1 These estimates are based on information from local residents. The first verson of this ethnographic account appeared in *Rajasthan Journal of Sociology*, No. 13, October 2021.

2 Surinder S. Jodhka, 'Dissociation, Distancing and Autonomy: Caste and Untouchability in Rural Punjab', *Dalits in Regional Context*, ed. Harish K. Puri, New Delhi: Rawat, 2004; Ronki Ram, 'Social Exclusion, Resistance and Deras: Exploring the myth of caste less Sikh society in Punjab', *Economic and Political Weekly*, 6 October 2007; Mark Juergensmeyer, 'Ad Dharma Movement', *Social and Political movements: Readings on Punjab*, ed. Harish K. Puri and Paramjit S. Judge, Jaipur and New Delhi: Rawat, 2000; Singh 2020, Jodhka 2009.

3 In the Sikh tradition, there are only ten gurus. The other holy saints, while equally respected, are referred to as *bhagats*.

4 Singh, 2020.

5 See Judge 2010, pp. 29–46, for a detailed understanding of caste in Punjab.

6 Singh 1999, p. 13.

Chapter 2: Deras and Caste in Punjab

1 Avtar Singh Tehna et al, 'Kyon Banndey Hann Dera' (Why Deras Come into Existence), *Desh Sevak*, 3 June 2007.

2 Pashaura Singh, *The Bhagats of the Guru Granth Sahib; Sikh self-definition and the Bhagat Bani*, Delhi: Oxford University Press, 2003, p. 9.

3 N. Singh, 'Shiromani Committee and Caste', *Desh Sevak*, 1 July 2007.

Chapter 3: Dera Sacha Sauda: Manufactured Halo in a 'Little Fiefdom'

1 '2nd release in 2 months: Haryana government grants Dera chief 50-day parole', *Times of India*, 20 January 2024, https://timesofindia.indiatimes.com/city/chandigarh/2nd-release-in-2-months-haryana-government-grants-dera-chief-50-day-parole/articleshow/106998483.cms; 'Fresh furlough ahead of Rajasthan polls: Dera chief granted 3-week temporary release — 3rd this year, 8th in 3 years' *Indian Express*, 21 November 2023, https://indianexpress.com/article/cities/chandigarh/gurmeet-ram-rahim-granted-temporary-release-3rd-this-year-8th-in-3-years-9035824/.

2 Malwa comprises districts largely in the southern half of Punjab bordering Haryana and Rajasthan. Bathinda, Barnala, Sangrur, Mansa and a few other districts fall in this region. It is the largest region of Punjab. Doaba is the region between the rivers Satluj and Beas and comprises Jalandhar, Kapurthala and a couple of other districts. Majha largely comprises districts bordering Pakistan—Amritsar, Tarn Taran, Gurdaspur and Pathankot.

3 Lionel Baixas, 'The Dera Sacha Sauda controversy and beyond', *Economic and Political Weekly*, 6 October 2007.

4 'Sacha Sauda followers clash with police, 12 hurt', *One India*, 15 May 2007, https://www.oneindia.com/2007/05/15/sacha-sauda-followers-clash-with-police-12-injured-1179230904.html. This reference is merely illustrative. All the prominent newspapers such as the *Times of India*, *Hindustan Times* and *Tribune*, especially their Chandigarh editions, carried news of these developments in the state, beginning May 2007.

5 Anand Soondas, 'Look before you leap, Mr. Badal', *The Times of India*, 22 May 2007, Delhi/Chandigarh edition.

6 Manjeet Sehgal, 'Honeypreet, Vishwas Gupta were happily married for 11 years. Then came papaji', *India Today*, 4 October 2017, https://www.indiatoday.in/india/story/honeypreet-insan-former-husband-vishwas-gupta-gurmeet-ram-rahim-singh-dera-haryana-police-1057327-2017-10-04.

7 Ajay Sura, 'Dera Sacha Sauda Chief Gurmeet Ram Rahim found guilty of rape, taken into judicial custody', *Times of India*, 26 August 2017, http://timesofindia.indiatimes.com/india/dera-sacha-sauda-chief-gurmeet-ram-rahim-found-guilty-of-rape-cbi-court-ruling-comes-after-14-years/articleshow/60221119.cms; Amitoj Singh, 'Ram Rahim Guilty Of Rape, 30 Dead, 250 Injured As Sect Erupts: 10 Facts', NDTV, 26 August 2017, http://www.ndtv.com/india-news/gurmeet-ram-rahims-100-car-convoy-heads-to-court-ahead-of-verdict-10-points-1741807; 'Ram Rahim Singh's supporters riot after rape conviction', Aljazeera, 25 August 2017, http://www.aljazeera.com/news/2017/08/ram-rahim-singh-supporters-riot-rape-conviction-170825114911486.html; Varinder Bhatia, 'Explained: Gurmeet Ram Rahim convicted in Ranjit Singh murder case, what next for Dera chief', *Indian Express*, 8 October 2021, https://indianexpress.com/article/explained/explained-gurmeet-ram-rahim-convicted-ranjit-singh-murder-case-7559832/.

8 Manjeet Sehgal, 'CBI to probe 400 cases of castration of Dera disciples', *India Today*, 24 December 2014, https://www.indiatoday.in/india/north/story/castration-of-dera-sacha-sauda-disciples-gurmeet-ram-rahim-cbi-probe-hans-raj-chauhan-punjab-and-haryana-hc-232587-2014-12-24.

9 'No Padma award for Gurmeet Ram Rahim, but gets doctorate from World Record University', *India Today*, 27 January 2016, https://www.indiatoday.in/fyi/story/padma-gurmeet-ram-rahim-doctrate-degree-world-record-university-305605-2016-01-26.

10 '"Honeypreet will now be known as . . ." Gurmeet Ram Rahim changes adopted daughter's name', *India TV News*, 26 October 2022, https://www.indiatvnews.com/news/india/honeypreet-new-name-ruhani-didi-gurmeet-ram-rahim-baghpat-dera-sacha-sauda-head-sirsa-latest-updates-2022-10-26-818960.

11 'Final SIT report on 2015 Punjab sacrilege cases puts blames on Dera Sacha Sauda', *New Indian Express*, 2 July 2022, https://www.newindianexpress.com/nation/2022/Jul/02/final-sit-report-on-2015-punjab-sacrilege-cases-puts-blames-on-dera-sacha-sauda-2472228.html.

Chapter 4: Dera Sachkhand or Dera Ballan: The Epicentre of the Ravidassia Movement

1 I accessed a number of publications for this chapter. Here is a list:
Sant Surinder Dass Baba Ji (Dera Sachkhand Ballan, Jalandhar), *AmritBani, Satguru Ravidass Maharaj Ji (Steek)*, Shri Guru Ravidass Janam Asthan Public Charitable Trust, Seer Goverdhanpur, Varanasi (UP), 2013. English translation by Shri Piare Lal.
Siri Ram Arsh (English translation), *Amrit Bani Satguru Ravidass Maharaj*
Kashinath Upadhyaya, *Param Paras Guru Ravidas* (Hindi), J.C. Sethi, Secretary, Radha Soami Satsang Beas, Dera Baba Jaimaal Singh, Punjab, 1983
Raju Raaj, *Shri Satguru Sant Ravidas*, Dheeraj Pocket Books, Agrawal Colony, Meerut

2 Surinder Dass Bawa, *Amrit-Bani, Satguru Ravidass Maharaj ji*, Shri Guru Ravidass Janam Asthan Public Charitable Trust, Varanasi, UP, 2013, first edition, p. 23

3 Ibid.

4 'Crores lost in two days of violence', *Indian Express*, 28 May 2009, Delhi/Chandigarh.

5 'Birs shifted out from 6 Ravidass temples', *Times of India*, 11 July 2009, Delhi/Chandigarh; 'Bir shifted out from Vienna temple', *Times of India*, 16 July 2009, Delhi/Chandigarh.

6 'Village tense after Bir replaced with photo', *Times of India*, 14 September 2009, Delhi/Chandigarh.

7 Surinder Dass Baba Ji, Amritbani, Satguru Ravidas Maharaj Ji (Steek), A dera Ballan Publication. 2013. Translation in English by Shri Piyare Lal, p. 20.

8 'Punjab Assembly Polls Postponed Over Guru Ravidas Jayanti, Voting Now on 20 Feb', Quint, 17 January 2022, https://www.thequint.com/elections/punjab-election/punjab-assembly-elections-postponed-by-a-week-voting-on-20-feb-now-ec.

9 I.P. Singh, 'Message to Dalits in Punjab CM Charanjit Singh Channi's sleepover at Dera Sachkand', *Times of India*, 28 January 2022, https://timesofindia.indiatimes.com/city/ludhiana/message-to-Dalits-in-channis-sleepover-at-dera-sachkhand/articleshow/89167868.cms.

Chapter 5: The Making of a Pilgrimage: Dera Ballan in Varanasi

1 Sant Surinder Dass Bawa Ji, *Amritbani Satguru Ravidass Maharaj ji (steek)*, Dera Sachkhand Ballan, p. 44.

2 Shri Babu Ram Gautam, *Guru Ravidas Ji ke Anmol Bhajan*, Gurudinpurwa, Baishanpurwa, Suratganj, Fatehpur, Barabanki, Uttar pradesh, Singh Computer, 2016.

Chapter 6: Myth of a Monolith: The Ravidassia Identity and Its Reality

1 Santosh K. Singh, 'Dalit Politics and its fragments in Punjab: Does religion hold the key?', *Economic and Political Weekly* Vol LIII No 35. 1 September 2018, pp. 32–36.

2 Bernard Cohn, *An Anthropologist among the Historians and Other Essays*, Delhi: Oxford University Press, 1987; Nicholas B. Dirks, *Castes of Mind: Colonialism and the Making of Modern India*, New Jersey: Princeton University Press, 2001; Arjun Appadurai, 'Number in the Colonial Imagination', *Orientalism and the Postcolonial Predicament*,

ed. Carol Breckenridge and Peter Van der Veer, Philadelphia: University of Pennsylvania, 1993, pp. 314–39.

3 Suraj Yengde, 'A giant of Ambedkarite movement passes away', *Hindustan Times*, 19 July 2023, https://www.hindustantimes.com/opinion/a-giant-of-ambedkarite-movement-passes-away-101689746393248.html.

Chapter 7: Songs of Protest and the Politics of Posters: Decoding Popular Cultural Expressions

1 Chitleen K. Sethi, 'Fighter Chamars in Beghampura', *Indian Express*, 17 March 2013, https://indianexpress.com/article/news-archive/web/fighter-chamars-in-beghampura/.

2 Mark Juergensmeyer, *Religious Rebels in the Punjab: The Social Vision of Untouchables*, Delhi: Ajanta, 1988.

Chapter 8: The Myriad Hues of Deras in Punjab

1 Manjeet Sehgal, 'Punjab and Haryana High Court stays Ashutosh Maharaj's cremation order, says state has nothing to do with it', *India Today*, 16 December 2014, https://www.indiatoday.in/india/story/ashutosh-maharaj-high-court-stays-cremation-231320-2014-12-15.

2 Ajay Sura, 'HC allows preservation of Ashutosh Maharaj's body in deep freezer, *Times of India*, 5 July 2017, https://timesofindia.indiatimes.com/city/chandigarh/hc-allows-preservation-of-ashutosh-maharajs-body-in-deep-freezer/articleshow/59452379.cms.

Bibliography

Appadurai, Arjun. 1993. 'Number in the Colonial Imagination'. In *Orientalism and the Postcolonial Predicament*, ed. Carol Breckenridge and Peter Van der Veer. Philadelphia: University of Pennsylvania, pp. 314–39.

Baba, Surinder Dass. 2010. *Jagatguru Ravidas Maharaj ki Pawan Jivan Kathayen* (Sacred stories of Guru Ravidass Maharaj Ji). Varanasi, UP: Shri Guru Ravidass Janam Asthan Public Charitable Trust.

Baixas, Lionel. 2007. 'The Dera Sacha Sauda Controversy and Beyond'. *Economic and Political Weekly*, 6 October.

Bingley, A.H. 1970. *Sikhs*. Patiala: Department of Languages, Punjab. Second edition.

Callewaert, Winand M. and Friedlander, Peter G. 1992. *The Life and Works of Raidas*. Delhi: Manohar.

Cohn, Bernard, 1987. *An Anthropologist among the Historians and Other Essays*. Delhi: Oxford University Press.

Copeman, Jacob. 2012. 'The Mimetic Guru: Tracing the Real in Sikh-Dera Sacha Sauda Relations'. In *The Guru in South Asia: New Interdisciplinary Perspective*. eds Jacob Copeman and Aya Ikegame. New York: Routledge, pp. 156–80.

Dirks, Nicholas B. 2001. *Castes of Mind: Colonialism and the Making of Modern India*. New Jersey: Princeton University Press.

Grewal, J.S. 1990. *The Sikhs of the Punjab*. Cambridge: Cambridge University Press.

Hans, Raj Kumar. 2016. 'Making sense of Dalit Sikh History'. In *Dalit Studies*. eds Ramnarayan S. Rawat and K. Satyanarayana. Durham: Duke University, pp. 131–51.

Ibbetson, Sir Denzil. 1983/1970. *Punjab Castes*. Punjab: Department of Languages.

Jodhka, Surinder S. 2004. 'Dissociation, Distancing and Autonomy: Caste and Untouchability in Rural Punjab'. In *Dalits in Regional Context*, ed. Harish K. Puri. New Delhi: Rawat.

Jodhka, Surinder S. 2009. 'The Ravi Dasis of Punjab: Global Contours of Caste and Religious Strife'. In *Economic and Political Weekly* Vol XLV. No. 24, 79–85.

Jones, Kenneth W. 1973. 'Ham Hindu Nahin: Arya-Sikh Relations. 1877-1905'. *The Journal of Asian Studies*. Vol. 32, No. 3. May, pp. 457–475.

Judge, P.S. 2002. 'Religion, Caste and Communalism in Punjab'. *Sociological Bulletin*, Vol. 51, No. 2. September.

Judge, Paramjit S. 2010. *Changing Dalits. Explorations Across Time*. Delhi/Jaipur: Rawat Publications.

Juergensmeyer, Mark. 2000. 'Ad Dharma Movement'. In *Social and Political movements: Readings on Punjab*, ed. Harish K. Puri and Paramjit S. Judge. Jaipur and New Delhi: Rawat.

Juergensmeyer, Mark. 1988. *Religious Rebels in the Punjab: The Social Vision of Untouchables*. Delhi: Ajanta.

Juergensmeyer, Mark. 1991. *Radhasoami Reality: The Logic of a Modern Faith*. Princeton: Princeton University Press.

Kapur, Rajiv. 1986. *Sikh Separatism: The Politics of Faith*. London: Allen and Unwin.

Lorenzen, David N. 1996. *Bhakti Religion in North India: Community Identity and Political Action*. New Delhi: Manohar.

Madan, T.N (ed.). 1997. *Religion in India*. Delhi: Oxford University Press.

Madan, T. N. 2003. 'Religions of India, Plurality and Pluralism'. In *The Oxford Companion to Sociology and Social Anthropology*, ed. Veena Das. Delhi: Oxford University Press.

Madan, T.N. (ed.) 2004. *India's Religions: Perspectives from Sociology and History*. Delhi: Oxford University Press.

Marenco, Ethne K. 1976. *The Transformation of Sikh Society*. New Delhi: Heritage Publisher.

Meeta and Rajivlocahan, 2007. 'Caste and Religion in Punjab, Case of Bhaniarawala Phenomenon'. *Economic and Political Weekly*. January, 42(21), pp. 1909-1913.

McLeod, W.H. 1968. *Guru Nanak and the Sikh Religion*. Delhi: Oxford University Press.

Oberoi, Harjot. 1994. *The Construction of Religious Boundaries: Culture, Identity and Diversity in the Sikh Tradition*. Delhi: Oxford University Press.

Omvedt, Gail. 2008. *Seeking Begumpura: The Social Vision of Anticaste Intellectuals*. Pondicherry: Navayana.

Pathak, Dev N. 2018. *Another South Asia*. Delhi: Primus Books.

Philip, A.J. 2003. 'All in the Name of Almighty: The Caste Divide at Talhan'. *Tribune*, 16 June, Chandigarh edition.

Pinch, William R. 1996. *Peasants and Monks in British India*. Berkeley: University of California Press.

Puri, Harish K. 2003. 'Scheduled Castes in Sikh Community: A Historical Perspective'. *Economic and Political Weekly*, Vol. 38, No. 26. June 28-July 4.

Ram, Ronki. 2004. 'Untouchability, Dalit Consciousness and the Ad Dharm Movement in Punjab'. *Contributions to Indian Sociology* (NS), vol. 38, No. 3. Sept–Dec.

Ram, Ronki, 2004 a, 'The Dalit Sikhs'. *Dalit International Newsletter*, Vol. 9, No. 3. October.

Ram, Ronki, 2007. 'Social Exclusion, Resistance and Deras: Exploring the Myth of Casteless Sikh Society in Punjab'. *Economic and Political Weekly*, 6 October.

Rodrigues, Valerian. 2004. *The Essential Writings of B.R. Ambedkar*. Delhi: Oxford University Press.

Ronki, Ram 2024. `Intersectionality of Deras, Social Capital and Conflict Formation: Dera Sacha Sauda as an Exemplar'. In

Journal of Sikh and Punjab Studies (GISS, NY), 31 (1 &2), Spring-fall 2024: 97–167.

Sethi, Chitleen. 2013. 'Fighter Chamars of Beghumpura'. *Indian Express*, 17 March, Delhi edition.

Singh, Joginder. 2016. *Religious Pluralism in Punjab: A Contemporary Account of Sikhs Sants, Babas, Gurus and Satgurus*. Delhi: Manohar.

Singh, Khushwant. 1999. *A History of the Sikhs*. Delhi: Oxford University Press.

Singh, N. 2007. 'Shiromani Committee and Caste'. *DeshSewak*, 1 July, *Sunday magazine*.

Singh, Pashaura. 2003. *The Bhagats of the Guru Granth Sahib; Sikh Self-definition and the Bhagat Bani*. Delhi: Oxford University Press.

Singh, Santosh K. 2011. 'Globalization and Religious Identity in India: Understanding the Subaltern Context of the Sacred'. In *Patterns in Philosophy and Sociology of Religion*, ed. Mihaela Gligor and Sherry Sabbarwal. Delhi/Jaipur: Rawat Publishers.

Singh, Santosh K. 2017. 'Deras as "Little Fiefdoms": Understanding the Dera Sacha Sauda Phenomenon'. *Economic and Political Weekly*. Vol. LII NO 37. 16 September, pp. 20-23.

Singh, Santosh K. 2017. 'The Caste Question and Songs of Protest in Punjab'. *Economic and Political Weekly*. Vol. LII. No. 34. 26 August, pp. 33–37.

Singh, Santosh K. 2017. 'Fluid Faiths of South Asia: Ravidassia Movement in Punjab, India, as a Microcosm'. In *Another South Asia: Questions, Rhetoric and Quests*. Delhi: PRIMUS

Singh, Santosh K. 2018. 'Dalit Politics and its fragments in Punjab: Does religion hold the key?'. *Economic and Political Weekly*. Vol LIII. No 35. 1 September, pp. 32-36.

Singh, Santosh K. 2020. 'From Syncretism to Split: Ethnographic Insights from a Socio-Religious Movement in India'. In *Religious Diversity in Asia*, eds. Jorn Borup, Lene Kuhle, Marianne Q Fibiger. Brill Series in International Studies in Religion and Society. Vol. 34.

Singh, Santosh K. 2021. 'Baba Farid-Sheetala Mata Mandir, Guru's footprints and the pond of Pandavas: Mapping the sacred geography of a village in Punjab'. *Rajasthan Journal of Sociology*. No. 13. October.

Singh, Santosh K. 2023. 'Deras, Dalits and Caste Politics in Punjab, Decoding the Channi Experiment'. *Economic and Political Weekly*. Vol LVIII. No 19. May, pp. 26-29.

Snehi, Yogesh.2019. *Spatializing Popular Sufi Shrines in Punjab: Dreams, Memories and Territoriality*. New York: Routledge.

Taylor, Steve. 2014. 'Religious Conversion and Dalit Assertion among the Punjabi Dalit Diaspora'. *Sociological Bulletin*. 63 (2), May-August, pp. 234–46.

Tehna, Avtar Singh et. al. 2007. 'Kyon Bandey hann Dera?' (Why deras come into existence). *Deshsewak*, 3 June, *Sunday magazine*.

Tripathi, Anurag. 2018. *Dera Sacha Sauda, and Gurmeet Ram Rahim: A Decade-long Investigation*. Gurgaon: Penguin Random House India.

Upadhyaya, Kashinath. 1983/2008. *Param Paras Guru Ravidass* (Most Revered Sant Ravidass). Punjab: Radha Soami Satsang Beas (Dera Baba Jaimal Singh Publication).

Zelliott, Elianor and Rohini Mohakshi-Punekar (ed.) 2005. *Untouchable Sants: An Indian Phenomenon*. New Delhi: Manohar.

Relevant Interviews and Articles by the Author

Divya Trivedi, 'Deras and Dalit identity', *Frontline*, 13 September 2017, https://frontline.thehindu.com/the-nation/deras-amp-dalit-identity/article9855385.ece.

Somya Lakhani, '"We hear about Kabir, not Ravidas. Why?"', *Indian Express*, 1 September 2019, https://indianexpress.com/article/express-sunday-eye/we-hear-about-kabir-not-ravidas-why-5950845/.

Anju Agnihotri Chaba, 'Guru Ravidass, his teachings are relevant even today: Prof Santosh K Singh', *Indian Express*, 27 February 2021, https://indianexpress.com/article/india/santosh-k-singh-guru-ravidass-teachings-7206919/.

Santosh K. Singh, 'Explained: The Ravidassia identity', *Indian Express*, 16 February 2022, https://indianexpress.com/article/explained/explained-the-ravidassia-identity-7775717/.

Santosh K. Singh, 'Dalit-Sikh? The sociology of caste in Punjab', *Deccan Herald*, 29 September 2021, https://www.deccanherald.com/opinion/main-article/dalit-sikh-the-sociology-of-caste-in-punjab-1035297.html.

Santosh K. Singh, 'Frozen numbers, fluid faiths', *Deccan Herald*, 15 July 2021, https://www.deccanherald.com/opinion/main-article/frozen-numbers-fluid-faiths- 1008701.html.

Index